HOW TO DEFEAT GIANTS AND WIN

—— THE ——

CHAMPION'S
MIND

HOW TO DEFEAT GIANTS AND WIN

—— THE ——

CHAMPION'S

MIND

BY:

DR. DAVID M. WALKER

VINE
PUBLISHING

Unless otherwise indicated, Scriptures are taken from the Holy Bible, New International Version®, NIV® Copyright © 1973, 1978, 1984, 2011 by Biblica, Inc.™ Used by permission. All rights reserved worldwide.

Scripture quotations marked (NLT) are taken from the Holy Bible, New Living Translation, copyright ©1996, 2004, 2015 by Tyndale House Foundation. Used by permission of Tyndale House Publishers, a Division of Tyndale House Ministries, Carol Stream, Illinois 60188. All rights reserved.

Scripture quotations marked MSG are from The Message. Copyright © Eugene H. Peterson 1993, 1994, 1995, 1996, 2000, 2001, 2002 by Tyndale House Foundation. Used by permission of Tyndale House Publishers, Inc., Carol Stream, Illinois 60188. All rights reserved.

Vine Publishing's name and logo are trademarks of Vine Publishing, Inc.

ISBN: 9781736748374 (paperback)
ISBN: 9781736748381 (e-book)

Library of Congress Cataloging-in-Publication Data
Library of Congress Control Number: 2022907320

Published by Vine Publishing, Inc.
New York, NY
www.vinepublish.com

Printed in the United States of America

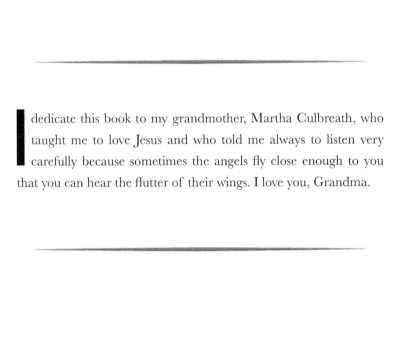

I dedicate this book to my grandmother, Martha Culbreath, who taught me to love Jesus and who told me always to listen very carefully because sometimes the angels fly close enough to you that you can hear the flutter of their wings. I love you, Grandma.

FOREWORD

Over the years, I have read over 1200 books and studied what it takes to be successful. I have worked with some of the most successful people on the planet, from professional and Olympic athletes to Fortune 500 CEOs. I have read countless biographies of successful men and women, each of them coming from different backgrounds, upbringings, religious beliefs, and starting points. And one thing is noticeably clear to me—your mindset is the starting place for all success.

In his new book, Dr. David M. Walker lays out the foundational truths it takes for any individual to begin their journey toward success and to dominate in life.

As you begin your journey toward success, you will be met with obstacles, problems, and situations, what Dr. Walker calls *giants*. However, in your hand is the tool you need to defeat those giants. Just as Dr. Walker recounts the biblical story of David and Goliath, this book becomes your slingshot and secret weapon to defeating the giants in your life.

In a skillful yet simplistic way, Dr. Walker lays out principles that the reader can implement into their life. This book is a tool that you should use over and over in your life to continue to defeat the giants that will arise from time to time.

Dr. Walker, your grandmother was right in naming you David; you are a mighty man and a giant slayer. Thank you for this gift that will help many slay the giants in their lives.

Outstanding job. Thank you for allowing me to be a small part of this masterpiece you have birthed.

~Dr. Will Moreland

Author of fifty books including, *Genius Potential*

CONTENTS

INTRODUCTION

I don't know how I'm going to win. I just know I'm not going to lose.
—*Author Unknown*

It was March 1960. Before sonograms or gender reveal parties, my mother, Shirley, was pregnant with me, her second child. The coming of a new arrival filled her and my dad, Melvin, with great joy and excitement. They did not know what gender I would be but they decided that they would name me Michael if they had a second son.

My mom was very excited and wanted to share the splendid news with everyone, but she made sure that her mother was among the first to know. So, several weeks before my birth, she visited my grandmother, Martha. My mom was wide-eyed and thrilled to reveal that she had finally come up with a name for her child. "Mom," she said, "If I have another boy, we're going to name him Michael." The news of the naming of her grandchild had captured Grandma's attention. At that moment, there was a sudden pause in their conversation. Then, total silence filled the room.

My grandmother was a small-framed woman, not at all intimidating. She was all of five feet tall, but her presence had an undeniable impact on our family. Her silver-gray hair and wire-framed glasses were the staples of her appearance. The small raised moles throughout her face were the map of her soul. Grandma was strong in her faith, and we always knew when she had been talking to God. Our family always shared major family decisions with her, and the naming of a grandchild was no exception.

So, after hearing the name of her grandchild, Grandma looked my mom directly in the eye and, with no hesitation or doubt, said, "His name will be David." My mother, shocked at what she heard, said, "It was like she never heard a word I said. All she said was, 'David will be his name.'"

Now, I'm not a mother, but I can't imagine someone else telling me what I should or shouldn't name my child. Could you? How would you have responded? What would you have said?

My mother replied, "But Mom, I like Michael." Grandma firmly repeated what she said. "His name is David, for in the Bible, David was the anointed king. David was also the one who killed Goliath, and David was a great man. My grandson, who will be named David, will be a great man." It was then that my mom realized that Grandma had a vision of what she saw for my life. Feeling exhausted by my grandmother's determination, she relented and asked, "Well, can his middle name be Michael?" Grandma, having a sense of satisfaction in her voice and knowing what God had told her said, "Yes, it can."

My grandmother saw my life through the lens of the biblical character King David, and the story of David and Goliath. If you grew in a religious environment, you most likely know the story or even heard it referenced during a sports contest. Sports announcers usually connect the fans to the story when an unbeatable champion faces an undersized opponent in a title match. Yet, the David and Goliath story also represents every person—"famous or unknown, ordinary or brilliant—who has faced an outsize challenge and been forced to respond."[1]

As far back as I can remember, I wanted to represent the biblical character well. As my grandmother said, David was the "anointed king"; he "killed Goliath" and was a "great man." While I was presented with a marker for success and set up to be a winner in life, I did not always feel I was a winner. I did not know who I would become. So, I struggled to live up to my potential.

Have you ever struggled to live up to your potential? Do you find yourself time and time again trying to figure out who you are? Do you ever feel defeated at times? If so, then I wrote this book *The Champion's Mind*, for you.

I wrote this book for people who want to win in the game of life. I wrote it for anyone who consistently face obstacles and challenges and wants to overcome them. Finally, I wrote this book for those leading teams and organizations who want to be more effective leaders.

So, the first thing I cover is how to master your gift. We all have received a gift from God designed to serve others and to bring prosperity to our lives. But, it's not enough to possess your skill. You must master it. I discuss the importance of being fearless and facing every crisis, knowing you are an overcomer. In this book, you will discover it's not enough to be an ordinary leader. You must be relentless in your pursuits with an attitude that says, "I will not quit." I also illustrate the necessity of knowing the art of communication. Whatever you do, in whatever field, results are best achieved when you communicate well. No one will listen to you if you don't know how to share your message. I also help you discover that your best asset is your character. There's nothing more remarkable than the integrity of character. You must be a person of your word. I discuss the significance of having a God-centered life. Finally, I cover how you must confront the personality trait within that can lead to failure. It can all fall apart because of your dark side. Learn how not to lose it all.

Each chapter provides principles and practical strategies for winning in life. At the end of each chapter, I offer action steps for you to follow. I suggest that as you read through the action steps, take notes, sit with it, grapple with it, and work through it. I know that as you read through the book and follow the principles provided, just like the shepherd boy who slew the giant and later became king, you will slay the giants in your life and win. Get ready to have your life changed. Get ready to become the winner you were born to be. Let's go!

GROWING UP DAVID

I was raised in Bedford-Stuyvesant, Brooklyn, New York. Bedford-Stuyvesant is the home of many notables, such as Earl G. Graves, Lena Horne, Chris and Tony Rock, the Notorious B.I.G., Jay-Z, Shirley Chisholm, Tracy Morgan, and George C. Fraser, to name a few.

Bedford-Stuyvesant in the 1970s was like most urban communities. Hard-working people comprised the neighborhood, but economic struggles were a reality for most families. I would not proclaim that Bedford-Stuyvesant was a poverty-stricken community, but abandoned buildings and vacant lots were visible on several streets. Drug-related crimes and gang violence were notable, which led many to live their lives cautiously with a watchful eye.

I was raised in a two-parent home with three of my seven siblings. My dad supported the family as a long-distance truck driver; he spent many days and nights away from home. He would call to see how we were doing and let my mother know he was doing well. He made sure to bring us treats like candy when he came home, and took us to the movies to make up for his absence. Later, he launched several entrepreneurial businesses, including owning a record store, a bus company, and becoming a gospel radio personality.

For most of the early years, my mother stayed home to meet her children's needs. Later, she spent some of her working years as a United States postal worker before leaving her career to support my dad in his business ventures. She worked tirelessly to keep her family together and to give us a future.

Both my parents were faithful churchgoers and had a relationship with Jesus, and they raised all their children to do the same. However, I want to credit my grandmother—who I mentioned earlier—as the most influential individual in my life regarding my spirituality, religion, and faith. She always told me it was essential to have a relationship with Jesus. Throughout my adolescent years, I spent a significant amount of time with my grandmother, who lived in Philadelphia, Pennsylvania. Sunday school, prayer meetings, outdoor tent gatherings, and church attendance all day Sunday were a must. I owe my spiritual foundation and much of my spiritual growth to the matriarch of the family.

During my high school years, I attended a school where the primary focus wasn't providing the best education for its students. School officials rarely discussed the importance of achieving good grades, graduating from high school, and progressing to earn a college degree. As a high school student, if you did not take responsibility for your education, school officials showed little interest in your well-being and academic achievements. In addition, both Black and White teachers taught us—consciously and subconsciously—that reaching goals outside the community was not essential. I believe this caused deeply-rooted psychological traumas in the lives of many young African Americans who lived in Bedford-Stuyvesant during the late 1970s and beyond. Fortunately, I graduated from high school and went on to higher education.

However, I struggled in the early years as a college student because of the lack of preparation in high school. As a result, I could attend college only if I agreed to take a full year of remedial courses before officially matriculating towards a degree. It wasn't easy, but I endured and overcame the challenge, and to date, I have earned several college degrees, including a doctorate.

After graduating college, I worked for many years as a New York City teacher and school administrator. More importantly, I returned to the same high school where I graduated and received some of my most significant educational challenges. I believed it was vital for me to give back to the community and help young African American boys and girls succeed in life. Later in my life, I had the esteemed pleasure of serving as a senior minister, providing spiritual development, economic empowerment, and social progress.for a culturally diverse congregation.

As I continued my life's journey, the story of David and Goliath always remained my favorite story of success, achievement, and winning against the odds. Then, one day, I made a conscious decision to revisit the story. I wanted to take a further look into David's life. I discovered that David was more than a king, more than a giant slayer, and more than a great man: David was a winner. He won every battle, defeated every enemy. He was a champion.

I researched what made David a winner. What caused him to defeat the giant Goliath and be a total winner in life? As I pored through the story of his life in the Bible, I found a scripture that shed light on this well-known biblical character's winning strategies: 1 Samuel 16:18. It read, "One of the young men spoke up, 'I know someone. I've seen him myself: the son of Jesse of Bethlehem, an excellent musician. He's also courageous, [a warrior], well-spoken, and good-looking. And God is with him.'"[2]

The Israelite nation had elected Saul its leader, although this was not God's desire for His people. Saul's outlandish behavior as a leader caused him to lose his position as king. His behavior displeased God, and He took away his authority. God also sent a dark, evil spirit to terrorize the king's soul as punishment.

In response, Saul displayed an uncontrollable behavior when the dark, evil, depressive mood was upon him. The king's servants needed to find someone who could play music well so the king would feel better when the evil spirit moved on him. One servant who heard and witnessed David's musical gift, told the king, "I know someone. I've seen him myself. He's an excellent musician.'" He also described David as courageous and one with a warrior mindset. In addition, David was well-spoken and distinguishable in his appearance. Lastly, he believed God was with David.

At first glance, the description in 1 Samuel 16:18 seemed insignificant to me, but as I studied the text, I realized that each character trait described was actually the leadership principles and practical strategies needed to win in the game of life. David uses each of these specific qualities and characteristics as a foundation to his success.

As you journey through this book, you will see how David's characteristics gave him the winning edge as he journeyed through life. I believe that you too can implement these leadership principles as a strategy for you to win. David's life remains highly regarded throughout the world as a shepherd, psalmist, and king. In addition, we know him as one of the greatest overcomers in history. So get ready to slay giants and achieve *The Champion's Mind.*

CHAPTER 1

Master Your Gift

"One of the greatest moments of a person's life is the skills they discover within themselves."

—*Tim Shockley Jr.*

L et me begin this chapter by making an undeniable claim: everyone has a gift. When I say the word *gift*, I mean a skill, a talent, or an ability that's personally yours and yours alone. Your gift is the "secret sauce" that makes you stand out from everyone else.

We were all born with a unique ability. That's you! That's me! No one is left out of having a unique skillset.

David's gift was as a musician. His expertise was playing the harp. He didn't just have the basic skills needed to play the harp; he was a master at his craft. His mastery at playing the harp was called upon to soothe King Saul's evil, depressive mood.

It is noteworthy at this juncture to point out that although God anointed and appointed David to be a future king, his first arrival to the palace did not come through an earthly royal dynasty or with any celebrated pomp and circumstance. David's first appearance at the king's court happened because Saul's servants summoned him to play the harp for King Saul. His skill and ability opened the door for David's entry to the place where he would later become king.

It's not enough to have a gift, then develop it to the point of mastery. You must know the purpose for your gift. What is it supposed to do? Let's look at how you discern the gift you were born with in the next section.

EVERY GOOD GIFT

God gives each of us the ability to succeed and serve others, but how do we discern those God-given gifts? Let's start here: James 1:17 says, "Whatever is good and perfect comes down to us from God." This is excellent news because God has given you a gift that's good and perfectly suits you. Your gift is unique to you and no one can have what you have. You and I were born with a gift designed explicitly for who we are and how we show up in the world. The talent born inside of us has a name. Celebrated author Dr. Will Moreland calls it your "genius potential." I interviewed Dr. Moreland on my podcast, *Beyond the Culture with Dr. David M. Walker*, and during our conversation he explained that everyone is born with a gift, an ability, a natural skillset that's their assigned "genius." He shared:

> *I was reading my Bible. I was led to a scripture in 1 Corinthians 7:7. The Apostle Paul was saying, "I wish that every man would be like me, but I realized that every man has their own proper gift." I pulled out my dictionary, and I began to really study that word gift, and I came across the word genius. It is a synonym for the word gift. As I began to research that word genius, I began to find out it wasn't this mystical thing that only a certain group of people had, like Aristotle, Sir Isaac Newton, Plato,*

Socrates, or Euripides. It wasn't just a certain group of people. I found out that every one of us who is born has genius potential. Then I started reading the science behind it. Even the science tells us that every child who is born comes to this world with a sense of genius.[3]

How's that? You and I were born with a sense of genius inside of us. Here's something else to grab hold of: Your genius is not tied to your IQ. Your genius is what you do that no one else can do like you. You were born a genius. Embrace it!

Now let's reconsider the question at hand: How do you discern the gift you were born with?

COME ALIVE AND GO DO IT

What do you find yourself doing the most? What are you passionate about? What comes naturally to you that others find challenging? What do you love to do so much that, if no one gave you any money for it, you would do it for the joy and the excitement it brings to you? These are some of the questions you could ask yourself to help discern the birth gift in you.

Usually, you can find the answer to what you do best by asking yourself this most important question: "What makes me come alive?" No doubt, David came alive when he played the harp, and when you can answer the question of what makes you come alive, you are on your way to discerning your God-given talent. Legendary scholar, theologian, and author of the classic book *Jesus and the*

Disinherited, Howard Thurman, said, "Don't ask yourself what the world needs. Ask yourself what makes you come alive and then go do that. Because what the world needs is people who have come alive."⁴ That's it! What the world needs is for you to come alive. When you come alive, you give the world the best of you. When you come alive, you share with the world your passion and your drive. So, come alive. Your success depends on it.

Now that you understand that you were born with a gift or a talent and must master it to have great success, you need to understand your craft's purpose. Why has God given it to you? What is your gift supposed to do?

This may sound strange to you, but the truth is, the main reason you possess the gift you have is to solve other people's problems.

Let's revisit our story. King Saul is possessed by an evil, depressive mood. When the spirit comes upon him, he displays uncontrollable emotions and behavior. You may have heard the term *unhinged*— Saul was unhinged. Saul's attitude brought him to a point at which the servants around him feared his emotional responses to every situation. The king's servants called David to solve the problem of the king's uncontrollable mood swings. When David played his harp, the music "would calm Saul down, and he would feel better as the moodiness lifted."⁵

You may be asking yourself, "whose problem am I assigned to solve?" The answer is found within your skillset. Look at what you do. Who responds to your talents? Who asks you for solutions because they see results in your life? What problem do you see that needs solving?

MINE, NOW YOURS

Most entrepreneurs and creatives first conclude that they have a problem that needs a solution. Soon after solving their problem, they discover that hundreds of other people have the same or a similar issue that needs solving. For instance, in the late 1990s, Jeff Hoffman, one of the founders and partners of Priceline.com/Bookings.com, shared how he missed an airline flight. He stood in a line at the airport for an hour, only to discover that he was asked to show his ID when he got to the counter and then given a printed paper boarding pass for his flight. Jeff turned and looked at all the other people standing in the same line, only to step up to the counter to receive a printed boarding pass as well. He thought it was "crazy" that he had stood in line for an hour to get a boarding pass, and more importantly, it had caused him to miss his flight.

At that moment, an idea developed in his mind. He shared, "I went home that Friday, and I took out a pen and paper, and I drew up [a design for] check-in kiosks."[6] For all of you who have checked in at an airport kiosk to speed up the process of getting your boarding pass, Jeff first solved his problem, and then he solved the same problem for millions of people around the world. With today's technology, you can download your boarding pass to a smartphone for a more straightforward process of catching your flight on time.

There are thousands of people who are always looking for

someone to solve the problem that they have. Look for them, or better yet, they'll come looking for you. You are the solution to their problem. You are the remedy for their pain. You must believe it.

WORKING THINGS OUT

Let me say it again: your gift is God-given, and each of us has one—or more than one, in some cases. Now, while the gift is yours and designed to solve other people's problems, it will not reach its maximum level of effectiveness without developing your skills. You must put your skillset under constant development. Your talents must consistently go into what I call the "preparation room." The preparation room is the place where we go to develop who we were born to become. It's where we try and try again until we have mastered our gifts. It's the place of invention and, often, the re-invention of ourselves.

So, how long does it take to develop your gift? What kind of time must you put in to become proficient or an expert at your craft? I'm certain that, for David to have had the skillset to provide the solution to Saul's crisis, he would have endured hours of practice or rehearsals. He would have committed hours, playing a song repeatedly until he had the right sound. There is no doubt in my mind that when he played the harp for King Saul, he hit the right note every time. That's how you know you are a master at what you do: you hit the right note every time.

Malcolm Gladwell, in his best-selling book *Outliers*, popularized the notion that it takes at least ten thousand hours of practice to master a skill. He called this the ten-thousand-hour rule.[7] Gladwell wrote, "Ten thousand hours is the magic number of greatness." What did Gladwell mean? What did he recognize? In theory, Gladwell suggests that to become the best at what you do and maximize your craft, you must practice hours upon hours until everything is correct, and you arrive at your maximum level of effectiveness. It just might take ten thousand hours to develop your gift.

To some of you, this may be a frightening task or seem like an impossible goal to reach. Look at it this way: I believe if you focus and commit to developing your skillset, the time you put in won't appear to be that difficult. Remember, you are doing what you love the most and what you are most passionate about. When your skill reaches its maximum level of impact, you will be grateful for the journey and, more importantly, highly rewarded.

THE BEST EXPOSURE: ISOLATION

It's one thing to know that you must put in the time to master your gift. It's another to understand the significance of taking the time to develop your gift in a private setting. Several scriptures in the Bible indicate—whether it's giving to the poor, praying for a friend, or fasting to live a better spiritual life—"what is done in private, the Father who sees it will reward you out in the open."[8] World-renown motivational speaker and best-selling author Tony Robbins put it this way: "It's what you practice in private that you will be rewarded for in public."[9]

When you talk to professional athletes, most will tell you that the most significant improvements to their skill development occur during the off-season and not when the games are played. The off-season is when athletes are away from fans and other distractions. It's during the off-season that they put in the time to develop their weaknesses and enhance their strengths as an athlete. Great athletes like Michael Jordan, LeBron James, Serena Williams, Tom Brady, Simone Biles, Tiger Woods, Arthur Ashe, and many more, developed their skills in the off-season, not during competition against their opponents. The results of their off-season workouts are seen during the following season, when they are back on the field competing.

David was not an exception to the rule. As a shepherd boy, psalmist, and harpist, he spent time alone to tend sheep and develop his craft. David had to be excellent at playing the harp because he developed his skills during his "off-season." David mastered his gift and the story tells us that he was "summoned" to the king's court as a result. When you master your gift, you will attract opportunities.

WHEN THEY SEE YOU

You may have wondered whether your gift will get you the exposure you desire. Whether we will see your talent and you take center stage, particularly after spending so many hours mastering your gift. Millions believe that they will remain unknown or their gift not recognized unless they crash the party to make a name for themselves.

That is not always the case. William Pettaway discovered legendary soul singer Toni Braxton. During an appearance on National Public Radio (NPR), Braxton said:

> *I got five dollars I borrowed from my dad, and I went to this gas station in Annapolis, Maryland. I had a plan. I was going to put three dollars in my gas tank and keep two dollars for lunch. And this gas attendant comes up to me, and he was staring at me. And I'm thinking, OK, a little weird. But then he says, all of a sudden, "Are you a singer? I've seen you sing around the city. I'm a producer, and I would love to do some demos on you." And of course, I'm thinking this is a line. He might be crazy. He works at a gas station. But sometimes in life, you're at the right place at the right time. You have to take risks. And it turned out to be legitimate.[10]*

Did you get that? A music producer saw her at a gas station. He recognized her and said, "I've seen you sing around the city." Well, the rest of the story is history. Pettaway signed her to a music contract. Braxton became one of the most celebrated soul singers in music history. Someone recognized her talent, and someone will remember yours.

So many people are wondering how the doors of opportunity will open for them. How will the people they need to know discover them and be willing to allow them to show their skills and ability? The answer is that someone will see your skill, ability, and talent, and it will get you in the door. Your gift will make room for you and bring you before prominent people.[11] Your gift will open doors for you.

OPPORTUNITY NOT LOST

Have you ever heard the saying, "Use it or lose it"? You probably have, but guess what? That saying does not apply to your God-given gifts. Your gift is yours for life. It's yours for you to succeed in life. You cannot lose your talent. You cannot lose your gift. In fact, the Bible says in Romans 11:29 (NLT), "For God's gifts and his call can never be withdrawn." Here's how it sounds another way: "God doesn't take back the gifts he has given or disown the people he has chosen" (ESV). Now that's a powerful statement. What God gives to us, he doesn't take back, no matter the circumstances. So you don't have to worry that you will lose your gift if you don't use it.

However, with that said, there is something that you could lose if you don't use the gifts that you have: you could lose the opportunity to succeed and be an agent of change for people all around the world. Myles Munroe, noted pastor and motivational speaker, had this message:

> *The wealthiest place in the world is not the gold mines of South America or the oil fields of Iraq or Iran. They are not the diamond mines of South Africa or the banks of the world. The wealthiest place on the planet is just down the road. It is the cemetery. There lie buried companies that were never started, inventions that were never made, bestselling books that were never written, and masterpieces that were never painted. In the cemetery is buried the greatest treasure of untapped potential.*[12]

When David arrived at the palace with the sole purpose of

playing the harp to calm King Saul's evil, depressive mood, Saul was pleased because David changed his emotions for the better. King Saul urged, "Allow David to remain in my service, for I am pleased with him."[13] From that day forward, whenever the evil, depressive mood would come upon Saul, David would play his harp. Relief would come to Saul; he would feel better, and the emotional rollercoaster he was on would cease.

What if David did not show up when called upon? We can easily see that King Saul would not have had his problem solved. He would have remained in the state he was in, even though a solution was available to make his life better.

Now let me ask you: What if you don't show up when called upon? What if you don't respond to the call to solve other people's problems or make their lives better when you have the solution? Your gift, just like David's, was designed to be the solution for what ails people around you. If you don't put your gift out into the world, then an opportunity is lost to change lives for the better. Get your gift out there.

ACTION STEPS

As I conclude this chapter, I have attempted to make it

perfectly clear that you were born with your unique gift. Your gift is your advantage in life. To help you discern your God-given gift, here are some specific action steps you can commence to bring out the champion in you.

1. Write down what you believe is/are your God-given gift(s).
   a. Remember, your gift is a skill you perform naturally with little effort.
   b. Visualize where you could use your gift the most.
   c. Make a list of where you could use your gift immediately.
2. Write down ways your gift can solve the problems other people are experiencing.
   a. Make a list of at least three strategic ways you can get this done.
   b. Think about the best ways to leverage your gift.
3. Enter the preparation room to perfect your gift.
   a. Find a quiet place to commune with your thoughts and seek direction.
   b. Consistently practice your skill until you've mastered it. If you're a writer, write every day. If you're a singer, take vocal lessons.
   c. Take a class or a course to enhance your

knowledge and skills.

4. Apply your gift.

   Now that you have taken the necessary time to discern what gift God has given to you, put your talent into action. Bring attention to what you do best by sharing your gift with the world. You will be pleasantly surprised at the thousands of people who will support you in what you do. Everyone wants to be on a winning team. Be the team leader by putting your gift out front.

Follow these action steps and let the world see your gift.

CHAPTER 2

Be Fearless

"The moment you give up is the moment you let someone else win."

—*Kobe Bryant*

I t's not surprising that conversations centered on a champion's mindset include discussions about fear, terror, or being intimidated by various circumstances. What I discuss in this chapter is no exception. Winning on the journey of life will include demonstrations of bravery, boldness, and fearlessness.

My lesson with fear came with an opportunity to work in a new school district. I was a school administrator in New York City. I had worked in that school district for over a decade, developing excellent relationships with my staff and loving the experience of working with students and educating young minds. Unfortunately, a conflict arose between the building principal and me. From my viewpoint, the working environment soon became untenable and challenging.

When a new job became available, I felt a sense of relief, and an exhilarating joy started to build within me about the new job opportunity. However, the fear of launching out into the unknown soon began to take over my mind. I'd be leaving a place where I knew everyone, and everyone knew me, and going to a place where every face and experience would be brand new. Quite frankly, I was afraid. Fear set in, and I thought of every possible reason to stay and not move on to the new school district. Fortunately, I settled my mind and pushed past my fears. I allowed myself to see the benefits that awaited me instead of letting comfort and fear rule my mind. This experience taught me that every success story is full of fear.

Goliath challenged David to a battle. The stakes were high; the winner would own everything the loser possessed. People around David told him he could not defeat Goliath. Goliath was enormous and a far more skilled fighter, and David had little chance to beat him. Simply put, the message was that the opposition was too significant to conquer. There was no possible way that David could win. Does this sound familiar? Have you ever been told this, or even convinced yourself that you could not win? Here's how David responded: He accepted the challenge because he was determined to win. Goliath stood before him as an undefeated champion. David stood before the giant, willing to give it the best he had to offer. With the sling and a stone in his hand, David hurled it at the giant, striking him in the forehead and killing him. David wins!

THE FEAR FACTOR

You and I have had moments when the obstacles we faced seemed too great to conquer. No doubt, there were times when the desire to quit had a firm grip and refused to let go. We've all been there. The journey through life comes with a human emotion designed to challenge and frustrate our ability to achieve success in our lives. What is this human emotion? Fear.

Fear is a natural emotion we all experience as we navigate through life. Whenever we seek new horizons or attempt growth opportunities, experiencing fear or anxiety is an unavoidable encounter. Mehdi Toozhy, in his book *Keys to a Fearless Life*, posits that "Fear can be defined as a vital response to physical and emotional danger. Also, fear is reported as a feeling that is first detected by our senses and then by the actions."[14] We all can agree that fear is the emotion we experience when we believe danger is present.

Whether it's launching a new business, buying your first home, getting married, or having your first child, new adventures are packed with anxiety and extreme concern about whether everything will work out well. We must overcome our fears if we expect to possess the desires of our hearts. It was clear that David was outmatched when he faced Goliath, but he pushed past any fear or doubt he had to accomplish his goal to be the victor in the battle.

SUCCESS IS FULL OF FEAR

Nelson Mandela once said, "I learned that courage was not the absence of fear, but the triumph over it."[15] There are no success stories that do not include moments when we are afraid. Every success story comes complete with a full-throttled dose of fear.

During a television interview, megamovie and television star Will Smith shared his skydiving experience for his fiftieth birthday. Smith said, "I'm really confronting all the things that I've ever been scared of, and I'm just finding this really exuberant freedom in life."

He went further to claim:

> *The daily confrontation with fear has become a real practice for me. You realize that the point of maximum danger is the point of minimum fear. There's actually no reason to be scared! It only just ruins your day. You don't have to jump. And then, at that moment, all of a sudden, where you should be terrified is the most blissful experience of your life, and God placed the best things in life on the other side of terror. On the other side of your maximum fear are all of the best things in life.[16]*

Facing your fear is the most crucial aspect of enjoying the time given on earth. Never allow fear to keep you from moving forward into unknown territory. All you ever wanted in life is on the other side of fear. Go for it!

The key to overcoming fear is to develop a fearless mindset. Michael Sloan, in his book *The Fearless Mindset*, argues, "Fearlessness isn't about learning how to ignore how you feel, rather it is a mindset that will empower you to learn how to move past your feelings of fear and achieve the things that you have always wanted to achieve."[17]

The key to your success is your ability to reject negative stimuli, focusing on the positive and moving past the feelings of fear you face every day.

STAY POSITIVE

In Philippians 4:8, you can find these words:

Finally, brothers and sisters, whatever is true, whatever is noble, whatever is right, whatever is pure, whatever is lovely, whatever is admirable—if anything is excellent or praiseworthy—think about such things.

This is my go-to scripture whenever I find myself dealing with moments of fear and doubt. This scripture reminds us to refocus during fear-filled times. Focus your mind on the things that are "true, pure and right." This is how we gain a positive mindset. With a positive attitude, you can quell feelings of fear as they attempt to overtake you and keep you from moving forward to achieve your goals.

Bryan Stevenson, renowned attorney and author of the critically acclaimed book *Just Mercy*, gives us a glimpse into what we can accomplish with a positive mindset. Stevenson experienced segregated schools as early as the first grade, growing up in a small rural town in southern Delaware. After the *Brown v. Board of Education* school desegregation decision in 1954, schools were formally desegregated. However, minds remained unchanged, and the practice of segregation continued throughout the education system and beyond. Black and White children played separately during recess times. Black children and their parents continued to use the doctor's office's back door, while Whites remained privileged to use the front door.

Stevenson's encounters with racism and prejudice fostered a passionate journey as a lawyer to "end mass incarceration for those who suffer the legacy of racial inequity."[18] Stevenson purposed to win relief for death row inmates who were wrongly convicted of crimes and sentenced to death. He believed that "society should choose empathy and mercy over condemnation and punishment."

In Stevenson's darkest days of fighting to win clemency for a Black man who was wrongly convicted in the state of Alabama, he maintained a positive attitude and a fearless mindset. He believed that righteousness would win out in the end. Stevenson recalled how this highly publicized death row case in Alabama caused him to receive bomb and death threats because "we were fighting to free this man who was so clearly innocent."[19]

Stevenson realized that he had an obligation to fight, push, and keep going, even when things became "difficult and challenging." He said, "I'm still persuaded that hopefulness is important and critical to our ability to change the world. I've always believed that, but now I believe it even more deeply."[20] To date, Stevenson has won relief for over 125 people on death row. Stevenson kept a positive mindset as he won the battle, one innocent death row inmate at a time.

LET GO OF NEGATIVITY

Have you ever wondered why, out of nowhere, negative thoughts come to your mind? Negative thoughts or negative self-labeling has the power to impede our success. Athletes often find themselves trapped, placing negative labels on themselves. They fear failing or making mistakes during competition. They also fear the criticism of coaches and fans during games, leading to poor performance on the field. Usually, a poor performance happens when an athlete constantly focuses on negative thoughts, especially when not performing to the best of their ability.

International soccer star Ryan Fraser battled negative thoughts during competition.[21] In a highly-contested match with the game nearing its conclusion and the score tied, the ball was in Fraser's control as he had an opportunity to go one on one with an opponent and possibly put his team in the lead if he scored a goal. Fraser chose to pass the ball to a teammate instead of being aggressive to win the game. When asked by a reporter why he was so timid on the play, he said, "I didn't want to lose the ball, and they run in and score." Fraser played it safe. He focused more on possible failure than on potential success. When you are a winner, you play the game aggressively. You play to win. When your focus is on possible mistakes or errors, you will play it safe, and more often than not, you may lose the game anyway. Negative thoughts produce negative results. Positive thoughts create positive outcomes.

That's how David played the game. He refused to let negativity empower his mind. Goliath questioned why his opponents sent out a young boy to fight him. After threats of negativity ("You're too small to fight against me"; "You will never defeat me"), David would not let Goliath's opinion of him detract him from his goal—to win the battle.

Each of us experience negative stimuli daily. Therefore, it is essential to address all the negativity that goes on in your mind. Why? Because your body and life will go where your mind goes. A negative attitude has one primary goal: to keep you from succeeding. Therefore, stay focused on your dreams and goals. Be fearless. That's the only way to win.

LOOK AHEAD TO THE PAST

The battle between David and Goliath remains one of the most notable biblical stories. The sling, the stone, and the giant's defeat remain etched in the minds of all who are familiar with the story. However, there are details of David's life that are overlooked—details that directly affected his win in the legendary confrontation. The vital steps David had taken in his past aided his future success.

When David was home tending to his father's sheep, his encounters with adversaries proved invaluable when it came time to fight the giant. David shared, "When the lion or the bear would come and carry off a sheep from the herd, I would go after him and strike him down and rescue it from his clutches."[22] He added, "When he rose up against me, I seized him by his beard and struck him and killed him."[23] David drew from his past victories. He envisioned that these experiences gave him the confidence and the fortitude to win when the obstacle was far more challenging. The small victories taught him everything he needed to know.

Many don't realize how crucial the small achievements from your past are for your future victories. Whether you're the kid who made her first sale with a lemonade stand and became a business owner, or you won the race for high school class president that inspired a political calling, all victories on a smaller scale lead to giant-size wins in the future.

David L. Steward, the founder, and CEO of World Wide Technology, Inc., knows all too well about the importance of small victories. In his book *Doing Business by the Good Book*, Steward shared his experiences of growing up in Clinton, Missouri—a small town about 250 miles southwest of Saint Louis. As a teenager, he lived through the turbulent, racially charged era of the 1960s. Steward said, "I vividly remember segregation—separate schools, sitting in the balcony at the movie theater, being barred from the public swimming pool."[24]

Despite living in a society created to oppress him, Steward persevered to graduate from Clinton High School in 1969 at eighteen years old. Although everything in society expected him to be a statistic, he graduated from Central Missouri State University with a B.S. degree in Business Administration. Each moment of perseverance—each minor success led to significant wins for Steward. "The adversities I encountered during my youth served as my training ground for hard times I eventually faced as a struggling entrepreneur."[25] Steward experienced many hardships during his youth and young adult years. However, these experiences helped him to develop character and taught him how to persevere. The degradation and unwanted existence of people like him prepared Steward for many racialized encounters he would undergo as he started his tech company.

Many thought Steward's ambitions to succeed in high

technology were far beyond his capabilities. Moreover, they resented him for attempting to enter a space that did not highly recruit African Americans. Nevertheless, Steward persevered as a business executive, reflecting on the warning he received from his mother that he should not let bitterness and resentment get the best of him, because those negative feelings were self-defeating and a vain attempt to delay the process.

Steward has grown World Wide Technology into a multibillion dollar company, ranked as one of America's largest private companies. The barriers Steward faced as a youth gave him the willpower and winning mindset to overcome the many obstacles he faced as he stepped into the world of technology.

Look back into your past. Don't overlook those small victories. Take the lessons learned from each success and let them give you the strength to know that you, too, can overcome every obstacle that awaits you and win. You might not think those small wins matter— they do.

ACTION STEPS

As I end this chapter, it's critical to know both the negative and positive stimuli that enter our psyche.

Positive thinking will increase your chances of achieving your goals. Conversely, negative thoughts will challenge everything you want to place in the winner's circle. To help you consistently conquer fear, here are some specific action steps you can take to ensure your victory.

1. Face your fears.

   Remember, David stood face to face with Goliath. Avoiding your fears will only make them seem more ominous. Whatever you are afraid of, face it head-on, and you'll realize that it isn't as unbeatable as you previously thought it would be.

2. Use your imagination to visualize success.

   Your imagination is one of the most remarkable powers you possess. It gives you the ability to be creative and not be limited by any barriers. You must imagine yourself accomplishing the goal you set out to achieve. Use your imagination to overcome every fear purposefully. Then, declare what you shall be.

3. Write it down.

   a. Gratitude list: Make a list of everything you are grateful for in your life. Nothing can overwhelm your mind when you make a list of the things you have already. This shows appreciation for where you are while waiting to get to where you are going.

    b.   Letter to fear: Take the time to write a letter to what makes you afraid, literally. Your words are powerful. What you are fearful of will listen to you. "Hello, Fear, I am no longer afraid to achieve my goals. I will succeed; it's my right to do so."

4.   Be more informed and seek help.

Become well informed about every situation. You will eliminate anxiety as you get more information. Find a mentor or support group. It's the right choice.

5.   Be realistic about the risk you want to take.

There's a difference between taking a risk and being risky. It's alright to take a chance, but don't be chancy. Ensure that the steps you want to take do not cost you more than you can afford to lose. Count the cost to see if you are making the right decision.

6.   Celebrate your successes.

What you celebrate, you are likely to repeat. I used this philosophy throughout my entire education journey. When I received an A grade, I celebrated.

When I passed a class, I celebrated. When I earned a degree, I celebrated. There is nothing like the exhilaration you feel when you win. Celebrate—you deserve it.

Follow these action steps and be the fearless winner and champion you are inside.

CHAPTER 3

Relentless Leadership

"Demand more of yourself than anyone else can demand, knowing every time you stop, you can still do more."

—*Tim Grover*

Are you a relentless leader?

Has anyone ever asked you this question? Have you asked it of yourself? Relentless leadership is a critical component for your success. Relentless leadership is consequential when you are at the helm of an organization or group. If you are the CEO of a Fortune 500 company where you lead thousands of people and manage millions of dollars daily, it matters. It also makes a difference if you are a teacher who teaches a classroom full of students to build up their academic success to have a bright future. Relentless leadership plays a significant role for a mom or a twenty-first-century dad who runs the home to make sure it's organized and operates with precision, as best as possible. Relentless leadership matters, and it is an overlooked ingredient that is crucial to winning in the game of life.

Leadership is defined as an individual, group, or organization's ability to "lead", influence, or guide other individuals, teams, or entire organizations.[26] Kevin Kruse, author of *Great Leaders Have No Rules*, contends, "Leadership is a process of social influence, which maximizes the efforts of others, towards the achievement of a goal."[27] These examples make it unquestionably clear that leadership—at its best—influences and guides others to maximize potential and achieve designated goals.

So what does it mean when you are relentless in your leadership? Relentless leadership is the ability of a leader to take in stride objections to decisions made. Relentless leaders are determined to win and stare obstacles and challenges in the face, knowing that the opposition will not defeat them. They also keep moving forward, despite the setbacks that may occur. "Relentless leaders keep their eyes on completing the mission and are willing to find creative solutions when things don't go as planned."[28]

David was a relentless leader. He was a leader of men; a warrior. He won each military assignment because of his determined leadership ability. Relentless leadership was a visible component in David's life, and if you are a determined leader, it must be visible in your life as well.

YOU LOOK LIKE A WARRIOR

By all accounts, David was a warrior—a fighter, if you will. His warrior mindset was central to his leadership. Numerous biblical scriptures point to how David led a band of mighty men in one victory after another through various wars with his enemies. At every turn, his focused mindset produced the same result—a win.

Winning against the odds is critical for a relentless leader. If anyone knows what it takes to be a relentless leader, it's General Colin Powell. General Powell is the former chairman of the joint chiefs of staff, the former secretary of state, and the first African American to hold such prestigious positions in the United States government. Powell was born to parents who immigrated to the United States from Jamaica. He grew up in Harlem and the South Bronx in New York City. The streets of NYC were often dangerous for Powell and his family. He said:

> *We kept our door and windows locked. I remember a steel rod running from the back of our front door to a brace on the floor so that no one could push in the door. Burglaries were common. Drug use was on the rise. Street fights and knifings occurred. Gangs armed with clubs, bottles, bricks, and homemade .22 caliber zip guns waged turf wars.*[29]

However, Powell purposed that he would not become part of that scene and rose above his circumstances. He decided what he experienced as a young man living in NYC would not overtake him, but he would use it as motivation to create a better future for his life.

Powell developed his leadership skills in the army's Reserve Officers' Training Corps (ROTC). Soon after, he entered the United States Army and served in the Vietnam War. After holding several posts in the government, including positions at the Pentagon and the National Security Council, Powell was nominated chairman of the joint chiefs of staff by President George H. W. Bush, and secretary of state by President George W. Bush. Both the national chairman's position and the State Department's foreign diplomat role called for

Powell to lead other military leaders and be the leading national diplomat to represent the United States.

LEADERSHIP IS ALL ABOUT PEOPLE

Powell was a relentless and compassionate leader during his field military career. Winning military operations—like Operation Desert Storm in Iraq—against foreign nations was a significant achievement for Powell and the USA. When asked what it meant to win against an adversary, Powell proclaimed, "Like any football or basketball coach, you always believe you're going to win." He believed a winning attitude was vital no matter the circumstances or the operation's outcome. "I think whether you're having setbacks or not, the role of a leader is to always display a winning attitude."[30] A relentless mindset produced significant results in Powell's leadership.

Furthermore, Powell believed that good leadership was about the men and women he led on the battlefield. Powell made it clear that he was always happiest when he was in the field, leading and serving in army divisions. He declared, "Leadership is all about people. It is not about organizations. It is not about plans. It is not about strategies. It is all about people—motivating people to get the job done. You have to be people-centered."[31] General Powell led the United States Army's men and women as a warrior, as a fighter.

Relentless leadership is critical to your success in life. It's not more essential than anyone else's role on the team. However, it is crucial to understand that relentless leadership "is about impact, influence, and inspiration."[32]

I began this chapter by asking the question "Are you a relentless leader?" Have you answered the question yet? The success you desire can only happen when you become so determined to achieve your goals that nothing will stop you from claiming what's rightfully yours. Remember, you must keep your eyes on completing the mission and always be ready to find creative solutions whenever there's opposition to your planned goals. You can do it. It's in you.

EAGER TO FIGHT

So, back to the story of David and Goliath. If you recall, Goliath challenged Israel's troops to choose someone to fight with him. If Israel's selected challenger defeated Goliath, then the Philistine army would surrender to the Israelites. However, if Goliath won the battle, the Philistine nation would subjugate Israel. All the men of Israel's military were unquestionably afraid of the ominous threat that Goliath projected. Therefore, no one was willing to step forward and accept Goliath's challenge.

King Saul announced an incentive for any man who killed Goliath—a cash reward, his daughter in marriage, and a permanent tax exemption. David overheard the conversation. He asked what he could expect for killing the giant. David wanted to know the reward he would receive if he accepted the challenge and won. Yes. He was eager to fight.

The questions I propose to you at this juncture are: "What are you eager to fight for? What is so important to you that you are willing to go against the odds to have it?" When you're willing to fight, you show a keen interest, an intense desire, or an impatient expectancy for something you want. Simply put, it's when you want something so badly that you're willing to make every effort to go after it and fight for it. Let me ask you again: "What are you eager to fight for?"

Critically acclaimed author, world-renowned speaker, educator, and pastor Eric Thomas, better known as "E.T., the Hip Hop Preacher," gave us a profound observation into what it means to be highly passionate about success and willing to fight to the end to have it. He said, "When you want to succeed as bad as you want to breathe, then you'll be successful."[33]

What if I asked each of you, "How badly do you want to breathe?" No doubt, everyone would have the same answer to that question: badly. What if you were as eager to fight for your success as you are to breathe? How successful would you be? How relentless a leader would you become?

Whatever it is that you do and whoever it is that you lead, you must reach a point when you listen less to what is said about you, and less to those who tell you what it is that you should be doing, how you should behave, and how you are to feel about things. You must reach a level at which you let people judge you by your results—nothing more, nothing less. When you are a relentless leader, you never do things halfway or live with *could or should or maybe*. You "demand more of yourself than anyone else can demand, knowing every time you stop, you can still do more."[34] That's a relentless leader.

CONFIDENT, NOT SELF-CENTERED

Whether you are an aspiring leader, the leader of a large organization or the leader of a small group of people, the question is: "Do you have the confidence to get the job done?" Many leaders are known to be self-absorbed or self-centered in their governance of people. When they say, "I'm the boss," they mean it, and they make sure you know it. They're in charge of the operation and allow your opinion only upon request. Confidence in your leadership should be more about self-determination than your ego.

David was highly confident in what he could do. Whether he played the harp to soothe the evil, depressive spirit that tormented King Saul, struck Goliath in the forehead with a stone on his only attempt, or wrote all those beautiful poems that we call the Psalms of David. (I discuss David and the psalms in more detail in Chapter 4.) He was confident in what he did. David's leadership was more about others than himself.

The Bible gives us an excellent example of what it means to lead others without the necessity of ego-driven leadership: "Do not think of yourself more highly than you ought, but rather think of yourself with sober judgment, in accordance with the faith God has distributed to each of you."[35] The message here is that leadership is not about the leader's ego. Leaders should not see themselves as more significant than necessary, and certainly not more significant than the people they lead. They should be balanced, clear thinking, and wise—which is God's gift to them.

Relentless leaders who are confident within themselves understand that it's not about who they are or who they want to become. The measure of relentless leaders is more about wanting to inspire and motivate others to action by their vision and personal example, instead of using the power of their position to exercise control over the ones they lead.

LEAD TO FOLLOW

I've always been intrigued by a statement I heard many years ago by best-selling author and highly-acclaimed leadership coach John C. Maxwell: "If you think you're leading, but no one is following, then you're only taking a walk."[36] In several ways, Maxwell's thoughts sit at the heart of how to view leadership. Someone must be willing to follow your guidance. Otherwise, you're walking all by yourself and leading no one.

A relentless leader does not journey by themselves; it's an inclusive partnership between those who lead and those who freely follow. Author Brian Tracy suggests that the most effective manner of leadership is one that is without compulsion. "Become the kind of leader that other people would follow voluntarily," he expressed. "Even if you had no title or position."[37] I believe Tracy's comments reveal a central part of leadership—the free choice to partner with another. It's not about the leader's title or position; it's about how they make those who follow them feel about themselves.

VALUES ADDED

What makes a leader worth following? Thousands base their decision to pursue a leader on learning principles to make them rich, wealthy, or significant in society. The best choice for following a leader is the values a leader can instill in your life. Instead of asking everyone to follow them, leaders should ensure that they implant values into the lives of those who choose to follow them.

Two of the National Basketball Association's (NBA) greatest players and Hall of Famers, Kareem Abdul-Jabbar and Bill Walton, celebrated the relentless leadership of their college basketball coach, John Wooden. Wooden not only helped develop them as great basketball players, but he also prepared them for the game of life. Walton said of Wooden, "Of course, the real competition he was preparing us for was life. He taught us [the] values and characteristics that could make us not only good players but also good people."[38] Abdul-Jabbar offered his thoughts on Coach Wooden: "The wisdom of Coach Wooden had a profound influence on me as an athlete, but an even greater influence on me as a human being. He is responsible, in part, for the person I am today."[39] For each of these legendary athletes, Coach Wooden's leadership was far more about making them great men than great athletes.

Relentless leadership produces followers—followers who choose freely to journey the path with their leader. Followers who influence society because of the life values instilled in them.

FINISH WHAT YOU START

Relentless leadership is not measured by how well you launch the journey. If you look back at how you started your small business, entrepreneurial pursuits, or staffing your organization, many of you would say the journey began on unsure grounds. If not, you would at least say that unquestionably, you were not as well-organized as you hoped, but you started anyway. The good news about not starting as you had expected is that you're not measured by all the elements it takes to create the party, but by the fact that, at the end of the night, you're on the dance floor having the last dance. That said, it's critical to understand that it's not about your start, but how you finish.

Ecclesiastes 9:11 (ESV) and Matthew 24:13 (BSB) reminds us that "the race is not to the swift, nor the battle to the strong . . . but the one who perseveres to the end." The reward for fulfilling your destiny in life doesn't come from a quickly paced race or the physical strength you possess. It's about staying in the line until you get to the front. That's how you win.

I had the great fortune to attend a leadership development conference at which entrepreneur and CEO Jeff Fagin was the keynote speaker. Jeff detailed how imperative it is never to quit the race, but to ensure you stay in the line until you reach the front. "If you've made up your mind . . . that you want to become a world-class speaker, a world-class trainer, that's what you've decided you want to do, get in line and stay in line," he urged. "Eventually, the line keeps moving forward until you work your way to the front of the line."[40]

How many of you have had the great idea of starting a business or going back to school to earn a degree or have had some other burning desire, but in the end, you did not pursue it to completion? In plain language, you got out of the line. Staying in line is vital to your success. Many people spend their whole lives going from one line to another line to another line, believing they will reach the front in less time. Does this sound familiar? In fact, it takes more time to get to the front that way than if you stayed in the first line. Here's some advice: pick a line and stay in line, and when you get to the front, you can do whatever else you want to do. But don't quit; you're almost at the front of the line.

ACTION STEPS

As I close this chapter, I want to remind you that you are a relentless leader and should declare it to be so. To help you improve your leadership abilities, here are some specific action steps you can carry out to bring you into the winner's circle.

1. Have total confidence in your abilities.

   Leaders often doubt their ability to lead effectively. Maintain confidence in your leadership abilities so that you can pilot your team or organization through any challenges or obstacles that present themselves. Sometimes high-pressure situations arise. Face them with a determined will that you will win against all odds—even giant ones. Set at least five success goals and be confident you will achieve them.

2. Have creative thoughts and ideas.

   Creative thinking is critical to being a relentless leader. Critical thinking gives you the ability to be creative and not be limited by any challenges or unfamiliar scenarios. Think of at least three to five creative ways of accomplishing the goals you set out to achieve.

3. Inspire those you lead.

   Remember, as General Colin Powell said, "leadership is all about the people" you lead. Unite your team, group, or organization by identifying and sharing vision. Turning the vision into a team effort will show investment in the team and its role in the success of your organization. List ten specific actions you can take to inspire your team through a shared vision.

4. Commit to growth.

Leaders must develop leadership skills. Each month, commit to reading at least one or two books on leadership. Attend seminars, webinars, or training on leadership development. Your knowledge, confidence, and success will improve tremendously.

Follow these action steps and be what you are: a relentless leader.

CHAPTER 4
Effective Communication

"The art of communication is the language of leadership."

—James Humes

Have you ever been asked what message you want to bring out to the world, what you want to be remembered for doing or having said, or what legacy you want to create? These questions are best answered by understanding the critical reality of effectively communicating your message.

Communication is the way you transfer your message to the world. Communication experts have researched over centuries the most effective ways of communicating. The list goes from using your voice with its tone and pitch to using printed material such as books and magazines, and finally using body language.

David was described as "well-spoken." He was a person who was eloquent—an able speaker, gifted in speech, articulate, or intelligent in expression. David needed to communicate his message well, as communication is vital in all phases of leadership. Effective communication helps leaders gain trust, align pursuit of goals, and inspire positive change.[41]

LIFT EVERY VOICE

One of the more potent forms of communication is using your voice to get your message out and get your point across. King Saul and all his men were afraid of Goliath and never spoke a word in response to his challenge. They often spoke among themselves, but no one was brave enough to stand before Goliath and say what was on their mind. When you possess a champion's mindset, not only will you say what's on your mind, but you'll also say what you mean.

As David came face to face with Goliath, he was clear on what he wanted to say. There wasn't any doubt about the message he was sending. David spoke what was in his heart; he told Goliath what was on his mind. "You come to me with a sword and with a spear and with a javelin," David said to Goliath. "But I come to you in the name of the Lord of hosts." David stood firm in his message and was determined to identify its results. He further proclaimed, "This day, the LORD will deliver you into my hand, and I will strike you down and cut off your head. For the battle is the Lord's, and he will give you into our hand."[42]

Thousands of people are unsuccessful in their attempt to say what they will do and what they want. Speech communications coach Veronica Blakely explains when you have a message to get out, everyone should, "Have a point, make a point, and get to the point."[43] David's message was precise and straight to the point. He did not doubt in his mind he would win. He would be victorious, and that would be the result.

FINDING YOUR VOICE

The most important thing you must remember is that your voice matters, and your message matters. Before she was a voice in American literature, Maya Angelou's voice suddenly went silent at a young age for over five years. She experienced the horrific crime of being raped by her mother's boyfriend. Maya's voice identified her assailant. After a brief trial and a one-day jail sentence, authorities found the perpetrator beaten to death, purportedly at the hands of Maya's three uncles.

Horrified that her words may have caused someone's death, Maya refused to talk, and her voice became mute. "I thought my voice had killed him—so I stopped speaking," Angelou said in an interview.[44]

During these years of silence, Maya developed a strong memory of poems. She also watched as other church children sang songs and recited poetry. "I would sit in the children's pew and think, 'If only I could speak," she said. "And at thirteen, thanks to poetry, I did."[45] Maya was released from her prison of speechlessness to find her voice. She became world renowned as one of the most revered poets in history.

Finding your voice and speaking your truth is key to your victory. The world needs to hear your message. The only one who can share what you have to say is you. It's your voice. It's your message.

Although the message is yours, it's crucial to acknowledge that your message must meet people where they are and based on their needs. Far too often, the messenger is unwilling or unable to move from their world and speak on the issue within the listener's world. John C. Maxwell offers this advice: "If you want to get your message across, you have to learn how to communicate in someone else's world." Maxwell clarifies that the best way to have your message connect with any audience is to speak to their issues. "People don't remember what we think is important," Maxwell added, "They remember what they think is important."[46] Remember, your message must speak to your audience—in their world, in their language, and about their issues.

Finding your voice is sharing your message as God has given it to you. To make sure that your message gets out the way you want it to get out, you must be authentic and transparent and own who you are. Pretenders don't make it too far, and nothing wastes time more than a person trying to be someone who they're not deep down within themselves. Like David's message to Goliath, your core values and beliefs must be your priority, because nothing less will do. Be willing to stand against all odds, even if no one is standing with you because they are silent.

WRITE THINGS DOWN

A thought-provoking statement that I've heard over the years: "It's better to have a long pencil than a short memory." Simply put, it's better to write things down on paper than it is to depend on your mind to remember something that may be vitally important. As your voice has the power to express your message clearly and precisely, so does a written communication.

Communication is not limited to what we verbalize to one another. Putting pen to paper is another way of getting your message across. Messages written down can express your true sentiments and thoughts. Whether through a blog, a book, an email, or something as simple as sending a handwritten note (a lost art in the twenty-first century), writing your thoughts can leave a lasting imprint—sometimes for centuries after you are gone.

David communicated messages through his writing. He was a prolific writer. David is universally renowned for writing most of the psalms we find in the Bible. The psalms are sacred songs and poems intended to be sung and accompanied by a stringed instrument. Considering that David was a skillful musician (see Chapter 1), it suited him to be the author of most of the psalms. We can see David's poetic writing skills as he pens one of the greatest writing masterpieces of all times—the Twenty-third Psalm:

The Lord is my shepherd; I shall not want. He makes me lie down in green pastures. He leads me beside still waters. He restores my soul. He leads me in paths of righteousness for his name's sake. Even though I walk through the valley of the shadow of death, I will fear no evil, for you are with me; your rod and your staff, they comfort me. You prepare a table before me in the presence of my enemies; you anoint my head with oil; my cup overflows. Surely goodness and mercy shall follow me all the days of my life, and I shall dwell in the house of the Lord forever.

This Psalm has been quoted, sung, and played for centuries. King David wrote the Twenty-third Psalm to communicate to us that we should examine how God's grace and guidance are always with us when life is prosperous and things are going well. Additionally, David's message implores us to seek comfort from God amid moments of turmoil and tests in life.

No doubt the Twenty-third Psalm—and other psalms written by David—has been a blessing to you and many worldwide. Imagine that every day, your message about God's blessings was read and recited by millions of people. This would be a perfect example of getting your message out. Habakkuk 2:2 says we should write the message and make it plain so that those who come after can read and run with it.

UNDERSTAND TO BE UNDERSTOOD

It is imperative for leaders to communicate their message effectively. Multibillionaire investment mogul Warren Buffett believes leaders must take every step to communicate a compelling message. Otherwise, it's a losing proposition. Buffett suggests, "If you can't communicate and talk to other people and get across your ideas, you're giving up your potential."[47] How important do you think it is for Buffett to communicate effectively with the hundreds of businessmen and women he interacts with every day on Wall Street? Do you think it's essential for him to effectively communicate with the millions of investors who own shares in his company? What type of communication skills would he need to have to be the CEO of a major corporation with a personal worth of over $85 billion? Would you agree that developing your communication skills like Buffett would be worth the investment?

Effective communication is not an art you are incapable of mastering or maintaining if you mastered it previously. Author Brian Tracy declares that, "You can learn to communicate. It's like riding a bicycle or typing. If you're willing to work at it, you can rapidly improve the quality of every part of your life."[48] It's clear that once you learn to communicate well, it's easy to maintain, and it will assist you in your desire to be an effective leader.

Effectively communicating with your audience is crucial to your success, but hearing what your team, clients, and competitors have to say is also very crucial. Author Stephen Covey writes in his highly successful book, *The 7 Habits of Highly Effective People*, that you must seek first to understand, then to be understood.[49] In essence, effective communication is also about listening to what others have to say. Listening allows affirmation for the other person. Everyone wants to be valued and affirmed for what they have to say. Being a good listener will go a long way with those you are attempting to influence.

It's no secret that effective communication is vital to your leadership success. If you are unsuccessful at communicating effectively, you will not yield the desired outcomes from your business, organization, or in your general life. "Poor communication can only get you poor results."[50] When the results are inadequate or below standard, then success is an impossibility. Continue to strive to get your message out with clarity, precision, and accuracy. If you do, there can be only one result—you win!

ACTION STEPS

As I draw this chapter to its completion, effective communication is key to your success. To help you improve on getting your message out, here are some specific action steps you can enact to make an impact on the people around you.

1. Communicate for results.

   Communication is essential to your leadership. To communicate for results, know precisely what your message is. Don't make your message confusing, complicated, or hard to understand. Be precise and get to the point.

2. Write with clarity.

   Improvements to your writing require practice. Write a letter, an email, or a note every day to keep your writing skills current. Set a personal word count to achieve every day.

3. Read more books.

   Read all genres of books and other materials. Reading will expand your knowledge and vocabulary. Reading helps build analytical thinking and objective reasoning skills. Reading consistently improves writing skills. Commit to reading one or two new books a month.

4. Be a good listener.

   As I mentioned in this chapter, listening to your audience is another critical factor in effective communication. Practice taking time to listen to someone without commenting. Time yourself for at least one to two minutes without responding to the conversation. Take note of how you are improving.

Follow these action steps to effectively communicate with those you lead.

CHAPTER 5
Your Character

"Character, not circumstances, makes the man."

—*Booker T. Washington*

There's nothing better-looking than a person with character. In the most basic terms, a person with character has a respected name in conducting a transaction with others. Having character is a mainstay for those with a champion's mind. When David was selected to come to the palace, he was identified as having reddish hair, beautiful eyes and one who was "good-looking."[51] This description of David isn't only about someone who had long, wavy hair or bright rosy cheeks. David's selection as the right one for the job was because of his distinguishable appearance: his character.

CHARACTER IS DESTINY

A person with character possesses integrity, honesty, courage, loyalty, fortitude, and many other crucial virtues that promote good behavior. Moreover, a person with character will do the right thing because they believe it is the right thing. Author Jim Loehr, in his celebrated book, *Leading with Character,* suggests that our character is our distinguishable mark chiseled throughout our lifetime. In the simplest terms, it is the culture of behavior we create that best describes our character.[52] It is what we are known for and believed by many to be who we are in our inner being.

What would you do if you had an opportunity to get even with someone who wanted to do you harm? Let me be more specific. What would you do if someone tried to kill you, literally? That's what happened to David. King Saul wanted him dead.

Shortly after David's victory over Goliath, the relationship between David and King Saul became contentious. David's victory brought great joy to many of King Saul's servants. In their joyful celebration, they honored David's victory as more significant than any victory Saul ever had. They shouted that the king's greatest triumphs were in the thousands, but David registered tens of thousands in their eyes.

As you might imagine, their recognition of David did not sit too well with the king. King Saul became extremely jealous of David, to the point where he took every measure to take his life. The king launched a spear at David to kill him, but David escaped each attack. Saul also commanded his servants to look for David, and if they found him, they were to take his life.

One day, King Saul and his men were hunting for David when the king stepped into a cave to relieve himself. Unbeknownst to Saul, David was in the cave, lurking in the shadows. He could see Saul clearly, but Saul could not see him. The men with David suggested that his enemy was in his hand, and "you shall do unto him as it seemed good to you." They were suggesting that this was David's opportunity to kill the person who was trying to kill him.

David secretly cut off a corner of the king's robe. As David was leaving the cave, he called to Saul and showed him the portion of his robe he had cut off. David said, "See, the corner of your robe in my hand. I did not kill you, [so] you may know and see that there is no wrong or treason in my hands. I have not sinned against you, though you hunt my life to take it."[53]

Now, let me ask you this: Would you say that David's action was an indication of his character? I think so. David could have eliminated his opponent, and yet he chose to leave Saul in the hands of God. Our character is evident when we choose not to do what someone else has done—when we choose not to get even.

NURTURING THE SEED OF CHARACTER

So, how do you nurture your character? What does it take to build it up? When it comes to character, the truth is you express your character through the choices you make. Character is who you are when no one is looking. That said, to nurture or build up your character, you must assess yourself first.

What are your core values? It would be best if you defined what these values are and what they mean to you. What moral values do you feel the strongest about? You can measure your values by noticing what upsets you the most when you see it lacking in someone else. What do you see in others that strikes a chord with you? Now, I don't want you to sit in judgment of someone else's life. This question is to assist you with reflecting on what you value most in your life. To help you know your core values, create a list of what you love the most.

Put your beliefs into action. Good character is developed by what you do. The smallest of decisions made, even in less critical situations, can have a tremendous impact on your life or someone else's. You must live out your principles and values. When you live out your principles and values, decisions to do the right thing are easier to come by, making your character more consistent.

Who's in your circle of friends and colleagues? Surround yourself with people with high expectations and let them draw you toward living a life of high character. The more time you spend with others of good character, the more it will reflect in your actions.

Have you thought of spending more time with God to build your character? In Chapter 1, David isolated himself from everyone to develop his musical talents. Isolation is not only an excellent environment to increase your musical skillset, but it is also perfect for nurturing your character. When David was alone, God was his instructor. David spent an extensive amount of time listening to the voice of God to help develop his character. David focused on being a humble individual. Humility is central to one's character. Having humility shows that wisdom is in operation.

The building or nurturing of your character is a constant practice. It would help if you acknowledged where the deficiencies are in your personality and discovered ways to improve yourself. Developing your character positions you to win consistently in life.

WINNING THE RIGHT WAY

Character is the virtue we live by throughout our life, but character is also evident in our determination to win or survive. Carol Dweck, in her highly successful book *Mindset*, said that character is, "the ability to dig down deep and find the strength even when things are going against you."[54] The individuals whose stories I'm about to share demonstrate a particular strength of character that contributed to the world's betterment.

Wilma Rudolph

To have the best chance of winning the race of life, you need a good start out of the starting blocks. This was not the case for legendary Olympic track-and-field star Wilma Rudolph. Rudolph was born in Bethlehem, Tennessee, in June 1940. She grew up constantly experiencing illness and poor health. By the time she was four years old, she had suffered from several childhood diseases, including measles, mumps, chicken pox, and whooping cough. Since Rudolph grew up in the segregated South, the only nearby hospital was reserved for Whites only, so Wilma's mother had to provide constant care with home remedies.

Nearing her fifth birthday, Rudolph was stricken with pneumonia in both lungs, scarlet fever, and polio. The polio disease caused her left leg to twist to one side. Rudolph had to wear a brace on it for most of her childhood. The doctor's examination determined that there was no cure for polio and that if she survived the ordeal, walking would be impossible. "The doctors told me that I would never walk again," Rudolph wrote in her autobiography, "but my mother told me I would, so I believed my mother."[55] Wilma had an unwavering faith to survive what others said she wouldn't.

After overcoming her disabilities with her mother's love, great determination, and physical therapy, Rudolph played for her all-Black high school's basketball team. Soon, Rudolph was recruited by the track coach at Tennessee State University, who discovered she was a naturally gifted runner. In 1956, Rudolph, still a high school student, qualified for the summer Olympic Games in Melbourne, Australia. She was the youngest member of the US track-and-field team at the age of sixteen. She won a bronze medal in the 400-meter relay race.

In 1960, now a student at Tennessee State University, Rudolph competed in the Summer Olympic Games in Rome, Italy. After tying a world record with her time of 11.3 seconds in the 100-meter semifinals, she won the event with her wind-aided mark of 11.0 seconds in the final. Similarly, Rudolph broke the Olympic record in the 200-meter dash (23.2 seconds) in the heats before claiming another gold medal with her time of 24.0 seconds. She was also part of the US team that established the world record in the 400-meter relay (44.4 seconds) before winning gold with a time of 44.5 seconds. As a result, Rudolph became the first American woman to win three gold medals in track and field at a single Olympic Games. The first-class sprinter instantly became one of the most famous Rome

Olympic Games athletes and an international superstar lauded around the world for her groundbreaking achievements.[56]

Wilma Rudolph beat the long odds to become an Olympic champion. She displayed the character traits of resilience and perseverance, courage, devotion, and focus, amid several devastating illnesses. More than a half century has passed since Wilma triumphed in the Olympic Games. She is a shining example of perseverance and determination to push past any setbacks you experience in life. That's character.

Nelson Mandela

Nelson Mandela was the image of strength and resilience as he experienced unquestionable hardship and adversity as a prisoner in South Africa. During apartheid, the minority White rulership controlled the rights and freedoms of the majority Black citizens of South Africa. Mandela became increasingly involved in politics and joined the African National Congress. Later, he helped form the African National Congress Youth League (ANCYL) in 1944. Mandela rose through the ranks of the ANCYL, and through its efforts, the ANC adopted a more radical mass-based policy in 1949.

While fighting for all South African citizens' equal rights and standing opposed to the current regime, Mandela was arrested and placed on trial for sabotage in what became known as the Rivonia Trial. According to Mandela's autobiography, *Long Walk to Freedom*, he gave his famous "Speech from the Dock" during the trial. He memorized the final words of the speech, which has now become immortalized:

> *During my lifetime, I have dedicated myself to this struggle of the African people. I have fought against White domination, and I have fought against Black domination. I have cherished the ideal of a democratic and free society in which all persons live together in harmony and with equal opportunities. It is an ideal which I hope to live for and achieve. But if needs be, it is an ideal for which I am prepared to die.*[57]

Though Mandela's speech had a significant impact on the courtroom, subsequently, he was convicted and sentenced to life in prison. Mandela spent the next twenty-seven years locked up and confined to a small cell without a bed or appropriate plumbing. Because Mandela was a political prisoner, he was forced into hard labor, rationed smaller portions of food, and given fewer privileges than other inmates. Mandela was only allowed to see his family twice a year. Due to the inhumane conditions he experienced, it would have been more than understandable if he had given up hope for his freedom. However, that's not what Mandela did. Mandela was full of hope, not hate, and he was a man who was able to forgive his oppressors. He expressed, "Forgiveness liberates the soul; it removes fear. That's why it's such a powerful weapon."[58]

Still, Mandela remained determined throughout his imprisonment and created an international outcry against South Africa's racist regime. After twenty-seven years of imprisonment, Mandela's prison sentence ended. Upon his release, he acknowledged:

It is a great tragedy to spend the best years of your life in prison, but if I had not been to prison, I would not have been able to achieve the most difficult task in life, and that is changing yourself.[59]

Mandela added more: "I had that opportunity because, in prison, we have what we don't have in our life outside prison: the opportunity to sit down and think."[60] Mandela became an advocate—speaking consistently on behalf of his people. His voice created change and ended the White minority rule in South Africa. He eventually rose to become South Africa's first Black and democratically-elected president.

Nelson Mandela never faltered in his commitment to democracy, equality, and learning. Although on many occasions, Mandela was provoked to answer racism with racism, he never did. Nelson Mandela's life is an inspiration to the entire South African government and millions of people worldwide. Mandela is the epitome of leading and winning with character.

Pat Tillman

Would you give away your fortune and the fame of a celebrity to serve your country? When America needed Pat Tillman the most, he gave up everything to serve his country. Tillman provided one of the greatest lessons of real heroism, leadership, and character.

Tillman was a standout defensive back with Arizona State

University. Although he excelled in college, winning Conference Defensive Player of the Year, everyone believed that he was too small and too slow to play professional football.[61] That is, everyone except Tillman.

Tillman was drafted into the National Football League (NFL) by the Arizona Cardinals in the seventh round in 1998. He played four seasons, starting each game at the safety position. Tillman played his position so well that the Saint Louis Rams offered him $9 million to leave the Cardinals and play for their team. Tillman turned down the offer and stayed with the Cardinals because they had given him a chance when other teams wouldn't. Tillman took loyalty seriously. "He wanted to be the best football player he could, but much more important to him was becoming the best man he could."[62]

When the September 11 attacks took place, they struck a chord with Tillman. He took the attacks on our nation personally. He spoke with a reporter the day after the attacks, saying he had relatives who had fought in previous American wars, and he worried that "I really haven't done a damn thing as far as laying myself on the line like that. I have a lot of respect for those who have and what the flag stands for."[63]

Eight months after the attacks, Tillman wanted his agent to negotiate new contracts for his other clients. He decided he would enlist in the army and fight for his country. Tillman turned down a $3.6 million contract with the Cardinals to join the United States Army to become a ranger.

While stationed in Afghanistan, Tillman died from what

was ultimately determined to be friendly fire. Tillman received a posthumous promotion to corporal. He received a Silver Star Citation, which read in part:

> *His audacious leadership and courageous example under fire inspired his men to fight at great risk to their own personal safety, resulting in the enemy's withdrawal, his platoon's safe passage from the ambush kill zone, and his mortal wound. Corporal Tillman's personal courage, tactical expertise, and professional competence directly contributed to his platoon's overall success and survival. In making the ultimate sacrifice for his team and platoon, Corporal Patrick D. Tillman reflected great credit upon himself, the Joint Task Force, and the United States Army.*[64]

Pat Tillman's life exemplified humanity, sacrifice, and an enduring spirit. To many, Tillman possessed the character of a hero, a courageous and determined man willing to sacrifice his life for others. Pat Tillman was, indeed, a man of character.

ACTION STEPS

As I wrap up this chapter, I want to remind you that your greatest asset for winning in life is your character. To help you maintain awareness of how important your character is for your success, you can put some specific action steps into practice to keep you on the mountaintop.

1. Always be honest.

   Be honest about yourself. Your character reflects the values you maintain. Make a list of your core values. Put them on display for all to see. Be intentional to live by your core values in your interactions with your team and those you serve.

2. Be accountable.

   Who holds you accountable for your actions? Have an accountability partner for your business and personal life. Many protect one or the other—protect both.

3. Put your character on guard.

   As previously mentioned, your character is your greatest asset. Guard it at all costs. It takes time and effort to build it. You can lose it entirely with one wrong decision. Evaluate your friends and your choices thoroughly. Make necessary changes when these choices are not working out to your benefit.

4. Keep a journal.

Keep notes on the areas you are attempting to improve. Record your most significant obstacles and challenges. Record what steps you took to win despite them. Review your findings with your accountability partner. They will provide an objective review of your progress.

Follow these action steps, develop your character, and win.

CHAPTER 6
A God Presence

"Nothing in or of this world measures up to the simple pleasure of experiencing the presence of God."

—A. W. Tozer

"**A**nd the Lord is with him." This is how Saul's servant described David. What a powerful statement to have attached to your life! David's writing of the psalms, God's choice of him to be king, and God's acknowledgment of David—"A man after My own heart, who will do all My will"[65]—are powerful indications that there was a God-presence in his life.

Psalm 139 further illustrates the intimacy between David and God. In the verses, David reveals how God had thoroughly searched his life and knew his complete self. He also shares that God knew all his actions and thoughts and the words that he would speak. David declares that God was leading him and held him by the hand and directed his steps. He thoroughly enjoyed the love God had toward him and God's knowledge of all that existed around him. David confessed that God's presence was everywhere—no matter where he went in this life, God was with him. He knew that God's thoughts were abundant and precious. David concludes the psalm by sharing that God was faithful toward him, and His presence was ongoing.

GOD'S PRESENCE

What does it mean when there's a God-presence? That may not be as easy a question to answer. Millions of people around the world view God through multi-perspective lens. However, God's presence is all around us, as it was with David. God is a transcendent source in our daily lives. God is present with us by His eternal existence and is always affecting and influencing our lives.

In the presence of God is where we can find our deepest intimacy and communion with God. We know God, and God fully knows us. We are united. God is in us, and we are in God. In God's presence, we have the assurance that all is well, and God is working everything out for our good. God is in everything we do and involved with who we are to become. In God's presence, we build a relationship that allows us to put our trust in Him.

Life is filled with great uncertainty, pain, and misfortune. Despite this reality, having a deep sense of the significance of placing your trust in God is beneficial. Trusting God in matters that pertain to your leadership success is critical. Just like it was for David.

It is also crucial to trust God for your everyday living. It's essential to maintain a deep-seated belief that all circumstances—large and small—will arrange according to the higher good. David believed that, although he faced a formidable force in Goliath, with God's presence, he would be victorious—and so will you if you trust that all things are possible with God.

FAITH IN ACTION

Trusting God requires that you put your faith into action. Faith is not something that you can visualize, but it is yours to have. A scripture in the Bible says that faith is a "firm foundation. . . .It's our handle on what we can't see."[66] It's critical to acknowledge that it's not necessary to see your faith to know that it's real and that you have it. You must believe.

I had a recent conversation with a friend, Lawrence Smith. During our discussion, Lawrence shared a harrowing story of when his life was in the balance, and he faced near death. His experience illustrates his trust in God—even though he was still in his teenage years.

Early one morning, Lawrence was home with his younger siblings, and the house caught fire. He remembered being around thirteen years old and living in his grandmother's house because she had moved out to live in a senior housing facility. "We didn't have any furniture or anything," he said, "but we had the house because she let us stay in there, which was a good thing."

On that fateful morning, Lawrence recalled his mother left a pan of cooking oil on the stove and forgot to turn it off before leaving the house to look for a job. Lawrence and his siblings were asleep, but he kept hearing the smoke alarm go off. At first, he thought little of it because, as he recollected, his mother wasn't a good cook, and the smoke alarm had gone off on multiple occasions.

The alarm rang for about five minutes, and Lawrence wondered to himself, *What's she doing?* At that moment, he got up to see what was happening. When he walked into the kitchen, he could see smoke everywhere. Black smoke was all over the room. Lawrence's lungs quickly filled with smoke as he attempted to find good air to breathe. His siblings could hear him choking with every inhale.

Lawrence, straining to see through the black smoke, saw the massive fire over the stove. The fire was so big that Lawrence couldn't even put anything on it. "I just remember trying to get the fire out," he explains.

He remembered running into the room and getting his little brother out of the house. He then ran back in to get his sister out. He recalled, "I had to get everybody out of the house because they were so much younger than me."

After getting everyone out of the house, Lawrence ran to the next-door neighbor, banging on the door at five o'clock in the morning, trying to get someone to answer it. Finally, the neighbor answered the door and called 911. But the ordeal was not over for Lawrence and his family.

The truth is they lived in a low-income community. "In the projects, the police aren't coming anytime soon. Firefighters aren't coming anytime soon," Lawrence groaned.

When the firetruck arrived, thirty minutes had passed, and by that point, the family had lost everything. For months, Lawrence and his family were homeless with few options. Over time, Lawrence's family recovered from their loss and found a suitable place to live.

Reflecting on his experience, Lawrence shared, "It's scary to look back at it because it was like, how did somebody through all those things have faith, through all the things I went through, and still now go through?" Slowly shaking his head, Lawrence paused for a moment, then whispered, "How did that kid have faith at thirteen years old? To have had that faith back then in the situation where I couldn't write that story myself. That's scary, you know. I don't know. That's God."

Lawrence's story gives us a glimpse into what it means to trust that God is present no matter the circumstance. God's presence was a source of power and strength that helped Lawrence find the will to perform an act of heroism to save his family. Lawrence's determined will is a reminder of the saying "I can do all things in God's presence."

WALK IN THE SPIRIT

How would you define being spiritual? Being spiritual or having what some might refer to as spirituality is a broad concept that involves many different perspectives. It consists of finding peace, purpose and meaning for life, and feeling connected to a higher creational force. Being spiritual is also about the practice and outworking of the spirit and how it is developed, with its various aspects and relationships connected, sustained, and understood. Spirituality is relation- and action-centered, and is about making connections with these different aspects of life.[67]

Spirituality is found within the inner self in the presence of

God. For millions of people, being spiritual is the foundation for their existence. For example, former United States Secretary of State Condoleezza Rice suggests that spirituality is central to who she is and what she has become. She says,

Spirituality and faith are at the core of who I am. I was born to deeply religious parents who were able to give me that rock-solid foundation in the church and in my faith, which really has served me so well.[68]

Secretary Rice has been on a journey to deepen her spirituality. At times, she has struggled with it as her parents taught her to do, but also strived "not to become complacent" along the journey. They encouraged her to keep striving to bring forth her inner spirituality to the best of her ability. She has taken her spirituality with her all around the globe—it's her foundation. It should be yours as well.

Being spiritual also sits at the seat of our most outstanding achievements. It is through our spiritual understanding that we determine God's greatness for us. As world-renowned television talk show host Oprah Winfrey held, "It isn't until you come to a spiritual understanding of who you are—not necessarily a religious feeling, but deep down, the spirit within—that you can begin to take control." Ms. Winfrey's comments speak to the heart of the need to discern your calling and purpose in this life.

It is through God's presence that we are spiritual and that our spirituality exists. Since we have life by the spirit, it's incumbent upon us to order our lives every day through the spirit. The scriptures implore us to do so. "If we live in the spirit, let us also walk in the spirit."[69] In the presence of God, you'll find the fullness of joy and His entire will for your life.

VOICE OF MY PRAYER

If I were to ask you, "Do you pray?" I'm sure it is a question you can answer easily. If you have a relationship with God, there's no doubt you have prayed in God's presence. King David often was in God's presence through his prayer life. In one of his more special prayers in the Book of Psalms, King David is kneeling with his hands and head raised to God: "But truly God has listened; he has attended to the voice of my prayer. Blessed be God because he has not rejected my prayer or removed his steadfast love from me!"[70] David's prayer tells us that God hears our prayers. God knows who we are, and God is with us every step of the way.

As a doctoral research scholar,[71] I studied the religious and spiritual lives of Black male college athletes for my thesis. I wanted to know how Black male college students experienced religion and spirituality on their college campuses. Each student I interviewed expressed how they experienced the presence of God through their prayer life. They routinely petitioned God's help and assistance for success with classroom responsibilities, athletic duties, and other social affairs. One student (Jackie) sought guidance from God to help him endure his challenges. He did not want God to remove some of the problems he was experiencing, but he certainly wanted advice that would help him sustain his trials. Jackie contended that whenever he had challenging experiences, he would turn to God. "People are opinionated and want to try to give you the right advice and all of that, but sometimes that's not what you need. I like to talk to God about my problems." Jackie didn't want God to take his problems away but to help him make it through them. It was important to him to withstand stressful situations and not have them eliminated to make life easier. The students I interviewed fully witnessed God's presence. God's presence was instrumental in leading each student into living a productive and useful life within the campus community.

Prayer is our support when challenged with uncertain, stress-related circumstances. Additionally, prayer brings us into a deeper, more meaningful relationship with God. Your connection to God is your source of strength and helps you cope with the countless events you experience throughout your daily activities. A meaningful relationship with God is developed in God's presence through prayer.

ACTION STEPS

It's critical to know that God desires for you to be in His presence. To help you consistently maintain a direct connection with God, here are some specific action steps you can take to be aware of God's presence.

1. Meditate.

    Spend at least ten to fifteen minutes a day in silent meditation. You can use this time to clear your head of many life distractions. You can reflect on God's presence and be grateful for the many blessings you have in life.

2. Breathe.

    Center your mind on God and take several deep breaths. Exhale to relieve the built-up stress you incur in your mind and body. Inhale God's peace and feel His presence.

3. Read the Bible.

    Take the time to read the scriptures daily, especially when you need inspiration. You will experience the presence of God as you read and meditate on God's Word.

4. Have a conversation with God.

    There's nothing like having a conversation with God. Praying to God doesn't always have to be formal, like being on your knees or bowing your head with your eyes closed. You can maintain God's presence while taking walks during the day and having a simple conversation with Him.

God's presence is needed for success and to win in the game of life.

CHAPTER 7
The Dark Side

"...And David sent and inquired about the woman."

—*2 Samuel 11:3*

t was the time of year when kings were on the battlefield, but instead of fighting, King David decided to remain in the city. Feeling restless late one afternoon, he took a walk on the roof of the palace. Glancing over the rooftop, he noticed a woman bathing in her courtyard. Her beauty was striking, and she drew his attention. David wondered who this woman was.

The king asked his servants to find the answer. One servant answered, "She is Bathsheba, the daughter of Eliam, the wife of Uriah."[72] (Eliam was a member of King David's supreme military council. Uriah was a soldier who fought in the battle on behalf of the king.) David insisted that Bathsheba be brought to his chamber immediately.

Bathsheba found herself hurried to the king's chamber. She was unsure of the specific reason that the king had summoned her to the palace. When she arrived, David soon made his intentions known. He wanted to sleep with her—and he did. Weeks later, Bathsheba sent the king a message: "I'm pregnant." Shocked and amazed, David wondered what his next move would be. He thought it over. He had a plan.

David requested that the military commander send Uriah, Bathsheba's husband, home from the battlefield. In the king's mind, Uriah would come home and desire the intimacy of his wife. Bathsheba's pregnancy would then belong to her husband. David, however, did not anticipate Uriah's actions.

Astoundingly, Uriah refused to sleep with Bathsheba. He claimed a code of honor.[73] His fellow soldiers were still fighting the battle, and he would not enjoy the pleasures of his wife. After Uriah repeatedly refused to enjoy the pleasures of his wife, David again strategically thought of the best way to finally solve his problem.

Unable to cover his secret, David sent Uriah back to the battlefield, placing a letter in Uriah's hand to give to the commanding officer. "Put Uriah in the front lines where the fighting is the fiercest," the letter said. "Then pull back and leave him exposed so that he's sure to be killed."[74] The military commander obeyed the command of the king. Uriah died in the battle.

After hearing of Uriah's death, Bathsheba mourned her husband. When the mourning ended, David sent a servant to bring her to his house. David married Bathsheba; she gave birth to their son. The king's secret was now covered. So he thought!

TWO SIDES OF ME

In full view, we witness what might seem unimaginable for someone in King David's position. He had sex with another man's wife and then conspired to commit premeditated murder. Is this unbelievable?

David's story, as well as the stories I describe later in the chapter, may be astonishing to you, but the truth is there are two sides to every human being who lives on the face of the earth. There's the right side—the side that's in plain view. It's the side you see from a loving husband who adores his wife and children and presents an image of faithfulness and responsibility. There's the side of the teacher who educates the minds of her students. She is beloved and leaves a lasting imprint in all her students' hearts and minds, even after they become adults themselves. Millions of people in various occupations and positions—politicians, CEOs, athletes, and celebrities—daily present a side of themselves that represents what's good about all of us. However, there is a side that every person possesses. There is no exception to this truth. Everyone has a dark side.

In the first six chapters of this book, I provided fundamental principles and strategies to help you become a winner in life. In this chapter, I want to discuss the one crucial factor that most self-help and leadership-training books never discuss. Here's the reality: you will destroy the success story you created if you fail to control your dark side.

Tiger Woods

The name Tiger Woods became synonymous with the greatest players in golf in the early 2000s. He was young, brash, a phenom in the making who took the golf world by storm. He ascended to levels no other African American had attained before. He was a historic figure in golf.

Tiger won fifteen major championships, trailing only legendary golfer Jack Nicholas's eighteen major wins. Tiger was a highly sought-after commercial pitchman for companies such as Nike, Buick, Gatorade, and Tag Heuer timepieces—to name a few. In 2009, *Forbes* magazine celebrated Woods as the world's first professional athlete to reach over $1 billion in career earnings. Tiger was married. He and his wife had two children. Tiger's image around the world was that of a clean-cut husband and family man. Things soon took a drastic turn in Tiger's world.

In November 2009, the *National Enquirer* published a story claiming Woods had an extramarital affair with a New York City nightclub manager.[75] Soon after, more than a dozen women claimed in various media outlets to have had affairs with Woods.[76] This news rocked the sports world. It caused many men and women who had previously admired Tiger to shake their heads in disbelief about how he could have fooled them with the image that everyone wanted to see: wealthy, respectable, and responsible.

Woods called a press conference. He needed to address the barrage of media reports that had spread around the world. Millions of people watched the press conference. Tiger stood stoically in front of the cameras. Camera flashes bounced off his face as reporters jockeyed for position to assure their microphones and notepads captured every word that Tiger Woods would venture to disclose.

Tiger took responsibility for his actions. "I thought I could get away with whatever I wanted to," he lamented. "I felt that I had worked hard my entire life and deserved to enjoy all the temptations around me. I felt I was entitled."

Woods continued, adding that, "Thanks to money and fame, I didn't have to go far to find them. I was wrong. I was foolish."[77] Several companies ended their endorsement deals with Woods. He and his wife ultimately divorced. The once-celebrated golf champion had allowed the world to see what he had possessed all the while—a dark side.

Ephren Taylor

Ephren Taylor launched his first business, a video game development company, when he was twelve years old. "My parents weren't going to cough up forty to fifty dollars [for] a [video] game," he explained in an interview. As a joke, they told him, "Why don't you go figure out how to make one of your own?" With great interest, Taylor went to a bookstore, picked up a couple of books, and taught himself how to program. He said, "I got out a game, and some of the students at school thought it was worth ten dollars a disc, and I just started selling from there."[78]

During his mid-teen years, Taylor launched GoFerretGo. com, an online employment resource for teenage job seekers. The company grew to a value of more than $3 million. Taylor shifted his efforts to real estate, mainly buying property in depressed urban communities. His interest in socially-conscious investing led him to found Christian Capital Group. "We were basically going into urban communities," Taylor told the reporter, "taking housing and renovating it, and using the proceeds to fund churches and community organizations."[79]

Taylor later merged his company with City Capital Corporation and became its CEO. At the time of the appointment, Taylor was the youngest African American CEO of a publicly-traded company on Wall Street. Taylor's investment company attempted to build wealth in Black communities of faith. Taylor conducted a multicity Building Wealth Tour, during which he spoke to church congregations around the country and at various wealth-management seminars.

Taylor wrote several books and appeared on many TV shows, including on Fox News and CNBC, to expound on his cause. Taylor's career had taken him into information technology, real estate, and social activism. His activities positioned him as an inspirational role model and catalyst to help others understand and achieve financial success—at least until his dark side emerged.

In April 2014, Taylor was arrested and pleaded guilty in federal court to conspiracy to commit mail and wire fraud. In essence, Taylor's company was a Ponzi scheme that "targeted socially-conscious investors in church congregations."[80] Taylor epitomized a con game known as "affinity fraud." The US Securities and Exchange Commission describes affinity fraud as "investment scams that prey upon members of identifiable groups, such as religious or ethnic communities, the elderly, or professional groups."[81] According to the SEC,

Fraudsters who promote affinity scams frequently are—or pretend to be—members of the group. They often enlist respected community or religious leaders from within the group to spread the word about the scheme by convincing those people that a fraudulent investment is legitimate and worthwhile. Many times, those leaders become unwitting victims of the fraudster's ruse.[82]

At his sentencing, Taylor acknowledged that he had defrauded hundreds of investors of more than $7 million nationwide.[83] Taylor was sentenced to nearly twenty years in prison. After being told, "Do it yourself" by his parents, the kid who created a financial fortune could not build a protective wall between himself and his dark side.

IT'S NOT THE DEVIL; IT'S YOU

King David's escapades, as well as the behavior of the other lives highlighted in this chapter, demonstrate the indisputable reality of human life. We all have a dark side. The side of our personality that consists chiefly of primitive, negative human emotions and impulses like rage, envy, greed, selfishness, desire, and the striving for power.[84]

Several scriptures in the Bible help us understand that most of the undesirable actions we commit come from an inward desire. In a letter written to Christians living in Rome, the Apostle Paul reveals the truth of what we experience living this human life:

What I don't understand about myself is that I decide one way, but then I act another, doing things I absolutely despise. I decide to do good, but I don't really do it; I decide not to do bad, but then I do it anyway. Something has gone wrong deep within me and gets the better of me every time. It happens so regularly that it's predictable. The moment I decide to do good, sin is there to trip me up.[85]

In this passage, Paul acknowledges the desire within to behave contradictory to what was right. Thus, it shows that Paul is consciously aware of his dark side. Therefore, it's essential to take accountability for your actions and not blame it on something or someone else. Transferring the actions of one's dark side elsewhere, particularly to an unconscious level, does not resolve its effect; "it only makes the person more vulnerable to its increasing power."[86]

Jesus gives us further insight into our internal dark side. He said, "It's what comes out of a person that pollutes: obscenities, lusts, thefts, murders, adulteries, greed, depravity, deceptive dealings, carousing, mean looks, slander, arrogance, foolishness—all these are vomit from the heart. There is the source of your pollution."[87] Our main struggles and challenges come from within us. Jesus enumerates that it's from the heart that our words, affections, and desires proceed. No one is exempt from this fact.

Author William A. Miller depicts the "dark, undesirable, potentially explosive side of our personality" as our "shadow." In his enlightening book, *Make Friends with Your Shadow*, Miller helps us become acquainted with the inner part of who we are that "lacks balance and endurance."[88] Our dark side is that shadow.

We all have a side to our personality that can be unruly and often out of control. In an attempt to hide our dark side, we do our very best to present our "good and acceptable" face to the world, all the while hoping that no one sees what's truly inside. But, unfortunately, given the right, or some may say, the wrong occasion, our dark side will be exposed—unleashing the side we've tried to subdue, and uncovering the very thing we don't want to be, or want the world to see. Under these circumstances, many have proclaimed, "That's not me." But in fact, it is you.

Much like Apostle Paul's statement, I believe, "something has gone wrong deep within me and gets the better of me every time" encompasses the true nature of the dark side. But regardless, you must own your true self. You will never become your whole, authentic self, until you incorporate into your conscious self, the dark side of your personality.

"The devil made me do it", has been the response of millions of people when confronted with their transgression. But, these words are nothing more than an attempt to rationalize one's behavior and avoid personal responsibility for one's actions. Here's the truth, it's not the devil. It's you. Own it.

THE CHOICE IS YOURS

As leaders, we face the inevitable reality of making choices that could affect our lives. That's the choice to do right or do wrong; to live right or to live wrong. However, each choice we make comes with repercussions—and often unanticipated consequences. In King

David's case, God judged and punished him for having had an affair with Bathsheba and having her husband murdered. The child from David and Bathsheba's affair died, and God promised David that "killing and murder will continually plague your family."[89] Here, the repercussions were severe, and the consequences inevitable. No one is exempt from the results of their choices—neither you nor I, and certainly not the individuals we discussed in this chapter.

So, as you continue on your life's journey and come faced with your decision-making opportunities, the question is: Will you yield to the dark side or to the light?

ACTION STEPS

We must remain mindful of the dark side that lives in each of us. Owning our flaws, weaknesses, selfishness, nastiness, hate, lust, passions, et cetera, presents opportunities for growth and spiritual development in our lives. To help you consistently find the champion within, here are some specific action steps you can undertake to gain victory over your dark side and potential self-defeat.

1. Own it.

   Accept and embrace who you are and what your reality is. Owning your dark side leads to living a life with wholeness and balance. You're able to develop levels of maturity and become comfortable with yourself.

2. Develop self-awareness.

   Being self-aware assists with assessing feelings and reactions. Avoid unnecessary judgments and criticisms of yourself.

3. Be truthful and daring.

   A genuine and honest evaluation of yourself is essential. Bravely accepting those uncomfortable parts of yourself can be challenging. The rewards are worth the discomfort you may feel in opening new possibilities within you.

4. Write in a journal.

   Use a writing journal in which you can note discoveries you make in your life. Writing your thoughts and reviewing them can help you process the discovery into your awareness.

5. Meditate.

    Focus your mind on the acceptance of your humanity. Meditating can help you control negative thoughts and feelings. Take time to read the Bible and other books that help nourish and allow your authentic self to flourish.

6. Take full accountability for your actions.

    Seek forgiveness from God and everyone who you've wronged by your actions.

Follow these action steps to help you grow and be the winner that you are on the inside.

CONCLUSION

Execute The Plan

"You don't win on emotion. You win on execution."

—*Tony Dungy*

It was a Sunday afternoon. My hunger pangs screamed it was time to eat. So, I stopped at one of my favorite lunch spots after taking a walk through the neighborhood. I had visited the shop frequently, and the food was excellent. Two aspiring young entrepreneurs had started a business and were having tremendous success. They were living out their dream.

You had to be prepared to wait before you got your food. Customers filled the small space to overflow, wanting to eat good food on a pleasant Sunday afternoon.

Yes, I was hungry, but more than that, I wanted to stop by the shop and show my support for the business. I got to know Darius and Kai very well over a few months. Darius, an African American, was tall with broad shoulders. He always had a smile on his face as he enthusiastically attended to each customer. Kai was of Asian descent. He had a slight build, narrow shoulders, and a thin face. He talked a lot with his hands to make sure you heard every word of what he said.

I told them stories about me and my life's journey, and they told me theirs. We talked about family, career journey, and we discovered we had a mutual faith.

On this visit, as I stood in line, Kai saw me. He puts a smile on his face and then opens his mouth and, with a loud voice, he yells, "Hey, King David."

I turned to see the expression on the faces of those standing around. I wondered what they were thinking after hearing this announcement. I wondered whether they knew the story and who Kai was talking about.

In my mind, there was no doubt; Kai had just connected me again to David from the Bible. The same David who my grandmother had said was the anointed king, who killed Goliath, and was a great man.

Once again, there it was—that marker of success: King David!

At that moment, I could hear within my soul the very words my grandmother had said: "My grandson will be a great man." Instantly, I felt the winner in me. I felt like a champion.

Being a winner in life is not limited to having the name David or growing up with King David as your foundation for success like it was for me. No matter your name or who you are, you were born to win. God has given you all you need to overcome every giant obstacle that attempts to thwart your journey to reach the top of the mountain. There is no doubt about this.

As we conclude our time together, I want you to be sure of yourself and determined that you will live a life of success and achievement. Start each day by affirming that you are a winner and that you can do anything you set your mind to accomplish. Tell yourself there isn't anything that you are incapable of doing. Shout out loud: "I can do all things through Christ who strengthens me."

Affirm that there are no limits to your potential to conquer challenges and succeed.

Affirm that you will keep your attention on the goals and desires you have for your life.

Affirm that you have the power to create the life of your dreams.

Affirm that your life is full of joy and happiness.

Affirm that there is only greatness within you.

Affirm that you will embrace who God has made you.

So, now that you have all the leadership and success principles presented in this book, use them and win. Slay your giants and be your ancestors' wildest dreams, like I am for my grandma.

NOTES

INTRODUCTION

1. Malcolm Gladwell, David and Goliath: Underdogs, Misfits, and the Art of Battling Giants (New York: Little, Brown, and Company, 2013), 5.
2. 1 Samuel 16:18 (MSG).

CHAPTER 1: MASTER YOUR GIFT

3. Will Moreland, "Discover Your 'Genius Potential' with Dr. Will Moreland," Beyond the Culture with Dr. David M. Walker, https://podcasts.apple.com/us/podcast/beyond-the-culture/id1514211665?i=1000485586093, July 20, 2020.
4. Gil Bailie, *Violence Unveiled: Humanity at the Crossroads* (New York: The Crossroad Publishing Company, 1995), xv.
5. 1 Samuel 16:23 (ESV).
6. Jeff Hoffman, "What New Requirements Does the World Have?" (Conference presentation, Give Me the Mic, December 5, 2020).
7. Malcolm Gladwell, *Outliers: The Story of Success* (New York: Little, Brown, and Company, 2008), 39.

8. Matthew 6:4, 6, 18 (NIV).
9. Tony Robbins, "20 Inspirational Quotes that Will Help You Achieve Success," TonyRobbins.com. July 9, 2021, https://www.tonyrobbins.com/tony-robbins-quotes/inspiration-al-quotes/.
10. Toni Braxton, "Unbreak My Heart: Toni Braxton Gets Quizzed on Cardiac Surgery," interview by Peter Segal, *Wait Wait . . . Don't Tell Me!*, NPR, May 24, 2014, audio, 11:00, www.npr.org/transcripts/315236976.
11. Proverbs 18:16 (NASB).
12. Rachel Bridge, *Ambition: Why It's Good to Want More and How to Get It* (United Kingdom: Capstone Publishing, 2016), 3.
13. 1 Samuel 16:22 (NIV).

CHAPTER 2: BE FEARLESS

14. Medhi Toozhy, *Keys to a Fearless Life: Five Secrets to Overcoming Life's Greatest Obstacles* (Victoria, BC: Friesen Press, 2017), 5.
15. Cable News Network. "Mandela in His Own Words," CNN.com https://edition.cnn.com/2008/WORLD/africa/06/24/mandela.quotes/ (accessed July 12, 202).
16. "Bliss Is on the Other Side of Fear," Goalcast, accessed July 22, 2021, https://www.goalcast.com/2017/04/15/will-smith-bliss-other-side-fear/.
17. Michael Sloan, *The Fearless Mindset: Empowering Secrets to Living Life Without Fear and Worry* (Scotts Valley, CA: CreateSpace Publishing, 2016), 5.
18. Jean Case, *Be Fearless: 5 Principles for a Life of Breakthrough and Purpose* (New York: Simon & Schuster, 2019), 37.
19. One Lawyer's Fight For Young Blacks And 'Just Mercy'

October 20, 2014 3:00 PM ET Heard on Fresh Air https://www.npr.org/2014/10/20/356964925/one-lawyers-fight-for-young-blacks-and-just-mercy.

20. Darlene Ricker, "Justice, Mercy & Redemption: Bryan Stevenson, Founder of the Equal Justice Initiative, Has Learned You Can't Change the World Without Some Discomfort or Inconvenience," *ABA Journal* (August 2018), accessed March 12, 2021, www.abajournal.com/magazine/article/justice_mercy_redemption_bryan_stevenson/P2.

21. Patrick Cohn, "How to Overcome Negative Thinking and Beliefs," Peak Performance Sports, accessed February 22, 2021, www.peaksports.com/sports-psychology-blog/how-to-overcome-negative-thinking-and-beliefs/.

22. Gladwell, *David and Goliath*, 5.

23. 1 Samuel 17:35 (NASB).

24. David L. Steward & Robert L. Shook, *Doing Business by the Good Book* (New York: Hachette Book Group, 2004), 2.

25. Ibid, 98.

CHAPTER 3: RELENTLESS LEADERSHIP

26. Sonia Kukreja, Management Study HQ, How Good are your leadership skills?, accessed September 20, 2021, https://www.managementstudyhq.com/importance-qualities-good-leader.html.

27. Kevin Kruse, "What Is Leadership?" *Forbes*, April 9, 2013, www.forbes.com/sites/kevinkruse/2013/04/09/what-is-leadership/?sh=56d052b5b90c.

28. "Relentless Leadership," Wisdom Walks, www.wisdomwalks.org/148-blog/215-relentless-leadership.

29. Colin Powell, *My American Journey* (New York: Random House, 1995), 10.
30. Dan Schawbel, "A Conversation with Colin Powell: What Start-ups Need to Know," *Forbes*, May 17, 2012, https://www.forbes.com/sites/danschawbel/2012/05/17/colin-powell-exclusive-advice-for-entrepreneurs/?sh=27e27f1a6002.
31. Oren Harari, *The Leadership Secrets of Colin Powell* (New York: Mc-Graw-Hill, 2002), 125.
32. Robin S. Sharma, *The Leader Who Had No Title: A Modern Fable on Real Success in Business and in Life.* (London: Free Press, 2010), 57.
33. Eric Thomas, "Eric Thomas: When You Want to Succeed as Bad as You Want to Breathe." The School of Greatness with Lewis Howes, https://lewishowes.com/podcast/eric-thomas/, accessed June 25, 2021.
34. Tim Grover, *Relentless: From Good to Great to Unstoppable* (New York: Scribner, 2013), 5.
35. Romans 12:3 (NIV).
36. John C. Maxwell, *Leadershift Workbook: Making the Essential Changes Every Leader Must Embrace* (New York: HarperCollins Publishers, 2019), 186.
37. "Leadership Quote – Brian Tracy on Leading without a Title," December 3, 2020, http://www.leancxscore.com/leadership-quote-brian-tracy-on-leading-without-a-title/.
38. Carol Dweck, *Mindset: The New Psychology of Success* (New York: Ballantine Books, 2008), 208.
39. Ibid, 209.
40. Jeff Fagin, "Bigger than Any Challenge" (Conference presentation, Give Me the Mic, December 5, 2020).

CHAPTER 4: EFFECTIVE COMMUNICATION

41. Lauren Landry, "8 Essential Leadership Communication Skills," Harvard Business School Online, November 14, 2019, https://online.hbs.edu/blog/post/leadership-communication.
42. 1 Samuel 17:45–47 (ESV).
43. Veronica Blakely, "Present It and Quit it! - How to Give a Dynamic Presentation to Any Audience," Facebook, October 7, 2020, https://www.facebook.com/groups/BlackSpeakersNetwrok/posts/3243441832431896.
44. Tawnell Hobbs & Jeanna Cuny, "Finding Her Voice," The Shorthorn, February 27, 1998.
45. Gary Dowell, "Angelou Shows Passion for Education," The Shorthorn, April 4, 1995.
46. John C. Maxwell, *Everyone Communicates, Few Connect: What the Most Effective People Do Differently* (Nashville, TN: Thomas Nelson, 2010), 178.
47. Warren Buffett, *5 Communication Tricks Warren Buffett Used to Get Ahead*, May 1, 2017, https://www.cnbc.com/2017/05/01/5-communication-tricks-warren-buffett-used-to-get-ahead.html.
48. Brian Tracy, *No Excuses!: The Power of Self-Discipline* (Philadelphia, PA: Vanguard Press, 2010), 15.
49. Stephen R. Covey, *The 7 Habits of Highly Successful People* (New York: Simon & Schuster, 1989), 273.
50. Star Bobatoon, "'We Have a Failure to Communicate': The Power of Using Your Voice with Star Bobatoon," Beyond the Culture with Dr. David M Walker. https://podcasts.apple.com/us/podcast/beyond-the-culture/id1514211665?i=1000503399800, December 23, 2020.
51. 1 Samuel 16:12 (CEB).

CHAPTER 5: YOUR CHARACTER

52. Jim Loehr, *Leading with Character: 10 Minutes A Day to A Brilliant Legacy* (Hoboken, NJ: John Wiley & Sons, 2020), 12.
53. 1 Samuel 24:11(ESV).
54. Dweck, *Mindset*, 92.
55. "Wilma Rudolph," Biography, last revised January 7, 2021, accessed March 15, 2021, www.biography.com/athlete/wilma-rudolph.
56. Ibid.
57. Nelson Mandela, "Speech from the Dock," April 20, 1964, accessed March 21, 2021, www.nelsonmandela.org/.
58. Thomas Ashe, "Nelson Mandela" *Forgiving Prisoner,* December 11, 2013, https://blogs.shu.edu/diplomacyresearch/2013/12/11/an-exemplar-of-forgiving-prisoner-nelson-mandela/
59. Ashe, "Nelson Mandela."
60. Ashe, "Nelson Mandela."
61. John McCain, *Character Is Destiny: Inspiring Stories We Should All Remember* (New York: Random House, 2005), 82.
62. Ibid., 83.
63. Ibid., 85.
64. "Patrick D. Tillman," The Hall of Valor Project, accessed March 17, 2021, https://valor.militarytimes.com/hero/3912.

CHAPTER 6: A GOD PRESENCE

65. Acts 13:22 (NKJV).
66. Hebrews 11:1 (MSG).
67. Simon Robinson, "Spirituality: A Working Definition," in *Sport and Spirituality: An Introduction* (London: Routledge, 2007), 22–37.

68. Condoleezza Rice Quotes, Quotefancy.com, *https://quotefancy. com/quote/1382849/Condoleezza-Rice-Spirituality-and-faith-are-at-the-core-of-who-I-am-I-was-born-to-deeply*, accessed July 13, 2021.

69. Galatians: 5:25 (KJ21).

70. Psalm 66:19-20 (ESV).

71. David M. Walker, "An Examination of the Religious and Spiritual Experiences of Black Male College Athletes Attending Predominantly White Institutions: An Interpretative Phenomenological Analysis" (EdD diss., Northeastern University, 2019), 117.

CHAPTER 7: THE DARK SIDE

72. Eliam was a member of the King David's supreme military council. Uriah was a soldier who fought the battle on behalf of the king.

73. Code of Honor: It was typical for soldiers in preparation for war to abstain from sex as a practice of discipline.

74. 2 Samuel 11:14 (MSG).

75. "Tiger Woods Admits 'Transgressions,' Apologizes," Reuters, December 2, 2009, accessed January 23, 2021, www.reuters. com/article/golf-woods/update-4-tiger-woods-admits-transgressions-apologizes-idUSGEE5B11VL20091202.

76. Tim Dahlberg, "Two Weeks That Shattered the Legend of Tiger Woods," Associated Press, December 12, 2009, accessed January 23, 2021, www.post-gazette.com/sports/golf/2009/12/13/Tiger-Woods-Saga-Silence-that-sustained-golfer-is-shattered-in-two-weeks-and-nothing-will-be-the-same/stories/200912130201.

77. "Tiger Woods' apology: Full transcript," CNN, February

19, 2010, accessed January 25, 2021, www.cnn.com/2010/US/02/19/tiger.woods.transcript/index.html.

78. "Ephren Taylor Becomes America's Youngest Black CEO of a Publicly Owned Company: City Capital Corporation (CCCN)," Blacknews.com, June 18, 2007, www.blacknews.com/pr/ephrentaylor101.htm.

79. "Ephren W. Taylor, II," Contemporary Black Biography, Encyclopedia.com, accessed June 2, 2021, www.encyclopedia.com/education/news-wires-white-papers-and-books/taylor-ephren-w-ii.

80. "SEC Charges Ponzi Schemer Targeting Church Congregations," US Securities and Exchange Commission, April 12, 2012, www.sec.gov/news/press-release/2012-2012-62htm.

81. Affinity Fraud," US Securities and Exchange Commission, www.investor.gov/protect-your-investments/fraud/types-fraud/affinity-fraud.

82. "Affinity Fraud: How to Avoid Investment Scams That Target Group," US Securities and Exchange Commission, October 9, 2013, www.sec.gov/investor/pubs/affinity.htm.

83. Ephren Taylor, II, Pleads Guilty to Conspiracy to Commit Fraud, US Department of Justice, October 8, 2014, www.justice.gov/usao-ndga/pr/ephren-taylor-ii-pleads-guilty-conspiracy-commit-fraud.

84. Scott Jeffrey, "A Complete Guide to Working with Your Shadow," 2017, www.scottjeffrey.com/wp-content/uploads/Shadow-Work-Guide.pdf.

85. Romans 7:15–19 (MSG).

86. William A. Miller, *Make Friends with Your Shadow: How to Accept and Use Positively the Negative Side of Your Personality* (Minneapolis, MN: Augsburg Publishing House, 1981), 73.

87. Mark 7:20-23 (MSG).

88. Miller, *Make Friends,* Review excerpt on book cover.

89. 2 Samuel 12:10 (MSG)

BIBLIOGRAPHY

"Leadership Quote – Brian Tracy on Leading without a Title." December 3, 2020. http://www.leancxscore.com/leadership-quote-brian-tracy-on-leading-without-a-title.

Ashe, Thomas. "Nelson Mandela." Forgiving Prisoner. December 11, 2013. https://blogs.shu.edu/diplomacyresearch/2013/12/11/an-exemplar-of-forgiving-prisoner-nelson-mandela.

Bailie, Gil. Violence Unveiled: Humanity at the Crossroads. New York: The Crossroad Publishing Company, 1995.

Biography. "Wilma Rudolph." Accessed March 15, 2021. www.biography.com/athlete/wilma-rudolph.

Blacknews.com. "Ephren Taylor Becomes America's Youngest Black CEO of a Publicly Owned Company: City Capital Corporation (CCCN)." June 18, 2007. www.blacknews.com/pr/ephrentaylor101.htm.

Blakely, Veronica. "Present It and Quit it! - How to Give a Dynamic Presentation to Any Audience." Facebook. October 7, 2020. https://www.facebook.com/groups/BlackSpeakersNetwrok/posts/3243441832431896.

Bobatoon, Star. "'We Have a Failure to Communicate': The Power of Using Your Voice with Star Bobatoon," Beyond the

Culture with Dr. David M Walker. December 23, 2020. https://podcasts.apple.com/us/podcast/beyond-the-culture/id1514211665?i=1000503399800.

Braxton, Toni. "Unbreak My Heart: Toni Braxton Gets Quizzed on Cardiac Surgery," interview by Peter Segal. Wait Wait . . . Don't Tell Me! NPR. May 24, 2014, audio, 11:00. www.npr.org/transcripts/315236976.

Bridge, Rachel. Ambition: Why It's Good to Want More and How to Get It. United Kingdom: Capstone Publishing, 2016.

Buffett, Warren. 5 Communication Tricks Warren Buffett Used to Get Ahead. May 1, 2017. https://www.cnbc.com/2017/05/01/5-communication-tricks-warren-buffett-used-to-get-ahead.html.

Cable News Network. "Mandela in His Own Words." CNN.com. Accessed July 12, 2021. https://edition.cnn.com/2008/WORLD/africa/06/24/mandela.quotes.

Cable News Network. "Tiger Woods' apology: Full transcript." February 19, 2010. www.cnn.com/2010/US/02/19/tiger.woods.transcript/index.html.

Case, Jean. Be Fearless: 5 Principles for a Life of Breakthrough and Purpose. New York: Simon & Schuster, 2019.

Cohn, Patrick. "How to Overcome Negative Thinking and Beliefs." Peak Performance Sports. Accessed February 22, 2021. www.peaksports.com/sports-psychology-blog/how-to-overcome-negative-thinking-and-beliefs.

Covey, Stephen, R. The 7 Habits of Highly Successful People. New York: Simon & Schuster, 1989.

Dahlberg, Dahlberg. "Two Weeks That Shattered the Legend of Tiger Woods." Associated Press. December 12, 2009.

Accessed January 23, 2021. www.post-gazette.com/ sports/golf/2009/12/13/Tiger-Woods-Saga-Silence-that-sustained-golfer-is-shattered-in-two-weeks-and-nothing-will-be-the-same/stories/200912130201.

Dowell, Gary. "Angelou Shows Passion for Education." The Shorthorn. April 4, 1995.

Dweck, Carol. Mindset: The New Psychology of Success. New York: Ballantine Books, 2008.

Encyclopedia.com. "Ephren W. Taylor, II." Contemporary Black Biography. Accessed June 2, 2021. www.encyclopedia.com/ education/news-wires-white-papers-and-books/taylor-ephren-w-ii.

Ephren Taylor, II. "Pleads Guilty to Conspiracy to Commit Fraud." US Department of Justice. October 8, 2014. www.justice. gov/usao-ndga/pr/ephren-taylor-ii-pleads-guilty-conspir-acy-commit-fraud.

Fagin, Jeff. "Bigger than Any Challenge." December 5, 2020. Conference presentation, Give Me the Mic.

Gladwell, Malcolm. David and Goliath: Underdogs, Misfits, and the Art of Battling Giants. New York: Little, Brown, and Company, 2013.

Gladwell, Malcolm. Outliers: The Story of Success. New York: Little, Brown, and Company, 2008.

Goalcast. "Bliss Is on the Other Side of Fear." Accessed July 22, 2021. https://www.goalcast.com/2017/04/15/will-smith-bliss-other-side-fear.

Grover, Tim. Relentless: From Good to Great to Unstoppable. New York: Scribner, 2013.

Harari, Oren. The Leadership Secrets of Colin Powell. New York:

McGraw-Hill, 2002.

Hobbs, Tawnell and Jeanna Cuny. "Finding Her Voice." The Shorthorn. February 27, 1998.

Hoffman, Jeff. "What New Requirements Does the World Have?" December 5, 2020. Conference presentation, Give Me the Mic.

Jeffrey, Scott. "A Complete Guide to Working with Your Shadow." 2017. www.scottjeffrey.com/wp-content/uploads/Shadow-Work-Guide.pdf.

Kruse, Kevin. "What Is Leadership?" Forbes. April 9, 2013. www.forbes.com/sites/kevinkruse/2013/04/09/what-is-leadership/?sh=56d052b5b90c.

Kukreja, Sonia. "Management Study HQ, How Good are your leadership skills?" Accessed September 20, 2021. https://www.managementstudyhq.com/importance-qualities-good-leader.html.

Landry, Lauren. "8 Essential Leadership Communication Skills." Harvard Business School Online. November 14, 2019. https://online.hbs.edu/blog/post/leadership-communication.

Loehr, Jim. Leading with Character: 10 Minutes A Day to A Brilliant Legacy. Hoboken, NJ: John Wiley & Sons, 2020.

Mandela, Nelson. "Speech from the Dock." April 20, 1964. www.nelsonmandela.org.

Maxwell, John C. Everyone Communicates, Few Connect: What the Most Effective People Do Differently. Nashville, TN: Thomas Nelson, 2010.

Maxwell, John C. Leadershift Workbook: Making the Essential Changes Every Leader Must Embrace. New York:

HarperCollins Publishers, 2019.

McCain, John. Character Is Destiny: Inspiring Stories We Should All Remember. New York: Random House, 2005.

Miller, William. Make Friends with Your Shadow: How to Accept and Use Positively the Negative Side of Your Personality. Minneapolis, MN: Augsburg Publishing House, 1981.

Moreland, Will. "Discover Your 'Genius Potential' with Dr. Will Moreland." Beyond the Culture with Dr. David M. Walker. July 20, 2020. https://podcasts.apple.com/us/podcast/beyond-the-culture/id1514211665?i=1000485586093.

One Lawyer's Fight For Young Blacks And 'Just Mercy.' October 20, 2014, 3:00 PM ET Heard on Fresh Air. https://www.npr.org/2014/10/20/356964925/one-lawyers-fight-for-young-blacks-and-just-mercy.

Powell, Colin. My American Journey. New York: Random House, 1995.

Quotefancy.com. "Condoleezza Rice Quotes." Accessed July 13, 2021. https://quotefancy.com/quote/1382849/Condoleezza-Rice-Spirituality-and-faith-are-at-the-core-of-who-I-am-I-was-born-to-deeply.

Reuters. "Tiger Woods Admits 'Transgressions,' Apologizes." December 2, 2009. www.reuters.com/article/golf-woods/update-4-tiger-woods-admits-transgressions-apologizes-idUSGEE5B11VL20091202.

Ricker, Darlene. "Justice, Mercy & Redemption: Bryan Stevenson, Founder of the Equal Justice Initiative, Has Learned You Can't Change the World Without Some Discomfort or Inconvenience." ABA Journal. August 2018. www.abajournal.com/magazine/article/justice_mercy_

redemption_bryan_stevenson/P2.

Robbins, Tony. "20 Inspirational Quotes that Will Help You Achieve Success." TonyRobbins.com. July 9, 2021. https://www.tonyrobbins.com/tony-robbins-quotes/inspirational-quotes/.

Robinson, Simon. "Spirituality: A Working Definition," in Sport and Spirituality: An Introduction. London: Routledge, 2007.

Schawbel, Dan. "A Conversation with Colin Powell: What Startups Need to Know." Forbes. May 17, 2012. https://www.forbes.com/sites/danschawbel/2012/05/17/colin-powell-exclusive-advice-for-entrepreneurs/?sh=27e27f1a6002.

Sharma, Robin S. The Leader Who Had No Title: A Modern Fable on Real Success in Business and in Life. London: Free Press, 2010.

Sloan, Michael. The Fearless Mindset: Empowering Secrets to Living Life Without Fear and Worry. Scotts Valley, CA: CreateSpace Publishing, 2016.

Steward, David L. and Robert L. Shook. Doing Business by the Good Book. New York: Hachette Book Group, 2004.

The Hall of Valor Project. "Patrick D. Tillman." Accessed March 17, 2021. https://valor.militarytimes.com/hero/3912.

The School of Greatness with Lewis Howes. "Eric Thomas: When You Want to Succeed as Bad as You Want to Breathe." Accessed June 25, 2021. https://lewishowes.com/podcast/eric-thomas.

Toozhy, Medhi. Keys to a Fearless Life: Five Secrets to Overcoming Life's Greatest Obstacles. Victoria, BC: Friesen Press, 2017.

Tracy, Brian. No Excuses!: The Power of Self-Discipline. Philadelphia, PA: Vanguard Press, 2010.

US Securities and Exchange Commission. "Affinity Fraud: How to Avoid Investment Scams That Target Group." October 9, 2013. www.sec.gov/investor/pubs/affinity.htm.

US Securities and Exchange Commission. "Affinity Fraud." Accessed May 17, 2021. www.investor.gov/protect-your-investments/fraud/types-fraud/affinity-fraud.

US Securities and Exchange Commission. "SEC Charges Ponzi Schemer Targeting Church Congregations." April 12, 2012. www.sec.gov/news/press-release/2012-2012-62htm.

Walker, David M. "An Examination of the Religious and Spiritual Experiences of Black Male College Athletes Attending Predominantly White Institutions: An Interpretative Phenomenological Analysis," EdD diss., Northeastern University, 2019.

Wisdom Walks. "Relentless Leadership." www.wisdomwalks.org/148-blog/215-relentless-leadership.

ACKNOWLEDGMENT

I want to thank my Lord and Savior, Jesus Christ, for giving me the strength and endurance to complete my first book. To my wife, Emeline Toni Walker, you have been by my side for every significant achievement in my life. You have supported me and always made me feel that my successes were just as meaningful to you as they were to me. You accompanied me on this writing journey: reading, editing, and making sure that things were right. Thank you for believing in me. I love you very much, and I am glad that you agreed to take this life journey with me.

To my children, David Jr., Tameeka, Elizabeth, David III, and Navy Rose, you continue to be the light that shines brightest in my life. Everything I am motivated to accomplish in my life is because of each of you. I love you all very much.

I want to give special thanks to my family. To my siblings, I am grateful for the love and encouragement I received from all of you. To my late father, Reverend Melvin C. Walker, and mother, Shirley Walker, you are the guiding stars of my life. Your love toward me is the motivation that I have used to accomplish all my life's goals. I am forever grateful to both of you.

I want to extend special thanks to the members of my book committee. To Dario and Sherida Emans and my cousin Jonzell Holmes, your support through this process was the support I needed to accomplish this task.

I want to thank many of my friends of the clergy. To Bishop Norman Lyons, thank you for being a friend and a brother throughout my journey. You have always been there for me and encouraged me to achieve my highest goals. To Dr. Tyrone Stevenson, thank you for your spiritual insight. You helped me put the final touches on this book. To Apostle Jessie Edrington, you planted a seed many years ago that I would write books. I kept your words in my heart. Today, I am an author.

ABOUT THE AUTHOR

D r. David M. Walker is a former school administrator for the New York City Department of Education. He is a former pastor and a former NCAA Division 1 College basketball referee.

Dr. Walker earned a bachelor of science degree in secondary education, a master of science degree in sports management, and a post-master's degree in school administration and supervision from City University of New York-Brooklyn College. Dr. Walker is a graduate of New York Theological Seminary, where he earned a master of divinity (M.Div.) degree in theology. Finally, he received his doctor of education degree from Northeastern University, with a concentration in organizational leadership studies. Dr. Walker believes that education is the agent of a successful life.

Dr. Walker lives in Orlando, Florida, with his lovely wife, Emeline. He is the proud father of David Jr., Tameeka, and Elizabeth. He is grandfather to David III and Navy Rose. *The Champion's Mind* is his first book.

CPSIA information can be obtained
at www.ICGtesting.com
Printed in the USA
JSHW012257051222
34158JS00004BA/262